DEDICATION

This book is dedicated to the Almighty God for his numerous blessings in my life. He is my all in all and may his name be praised for ever.

I wish to appreciate my lovely wife and children for their unflinching support in making this a reality

ACKNOWLEDGMENTS

A big thank-you to every staff of M-I Nigeria Limited for your support, encouragement and love. Without mentioning names, you are all wonderful people and may God continue to bless you all.

To my darling wife, Helen Abiola. Her contributions are unquantifiable and invaluable. She is a virtuous woman indeed and I appreciate her contributions and inspiration

Thanks to Jacob, Peters and all other people who motivated me one way or the other in making this a reality.

Pst. C.E Ajufo, your contributions and guides are highly appreciated.

CONTENTS

1
Getting Started

Menu and Working Tools

Microsoft Excel 2007 is slightly different from the old versions of Excel. One of the problems often faced by users of Excel 2007 is their inability to locate some of the Excel functions due to the new layout. Unlike in the past, you don't see menu like File, Edit, etc. Below is the new look of Excel 2007 and where you can find some of your old menu items:

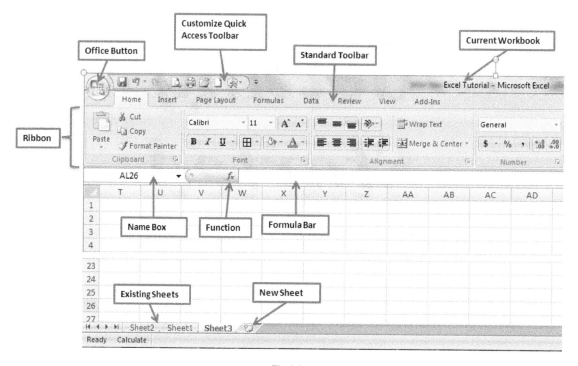

Fig 1.1

The first row on top has the Office button, the Customize Quick Access Toolbar, and the name of the workbook you are currently using. The Office button has most of the functions under File in the older version of Excel. Here is a screen shot of the Office button:

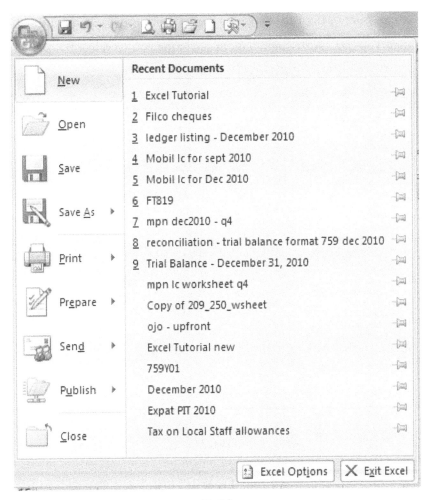

Fig 1.2

On the left, you have the menu options while on the right are the files used recently.

The buttons with arrows by the side indicate that there are sub-menu that can only display when you click the button. Here are some of the buttons"

Create a New File: There are basically two options available to users when creating a new file. Either click the icon under the Office [ ] New Toolbar or click the icon [ ] under the Customize Quick Access Toolbar. The icon under the Office Toolbar gives you more options than the Customize Quick Access Toolbar. It enables you to select from existing templates such as expense report, loan amortization, etc or create a blank workbook. A blank workbook is the only option under the Customize Quick Access Toolbar.

Open an Existing File: This can also be accessed through the Customize Quick Access Toolbar or Office Toolbar. A dialogue box appears for you to select the directory and your file name.

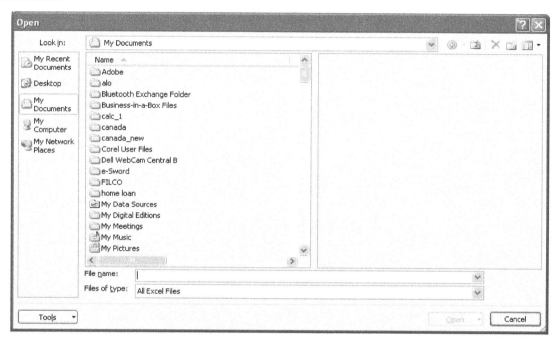

Fig 1.3

Locate the folder for your file under the "**Look in**" directory. The files of type display all Excel files and html files. You can change the format by clicking on the arrow besides "**Files of Type**" to select other files.

Once a file or folder has been highlighted, the "**Tools**" give you the options to delete, rename or change the attributes of the file or folder. You can also achieve this by pressing the right button of your mouse.

Save a File: Saves your file without prompting you for changes. This is very delicate especially when you don't intend to save changes made to a file. However, if you are dealing with a new file that has never been saved previously, a dialogue box will appear for you to type the name of your file.

Save a File As: Very valuable when you want to either create a duplicate or a different file format.

Print a File: This enables you to print your file. There are three available options under this menu:

a) <u>Print</u>: Allow you to modify your print parameters before sending your job to the printer. Print parameters include selection of printer, page setup, orientation, Printer configuration, etc.

b) <u>Quick Print</u>: Send your document to the printer without making changes using your most recent print parameters. If you have a print range setup already, the print range will be printed, otherwise, the entire worksheet will be printed.

c) <u>Print Preview</u>: Enable you to preview your document and make necessary adjustments before sending the job to the printer

Prepare: It enables you to prepare your document for distribution. You have the following seven options:

a) <u>Properties</u>: If you are planning distributing your document, it might be necessary to set the properties of your document. The properties include your name, your title, the subject, the keywords, category, status and comments. Below is a screen shot of properties:

Fig 1.4

b) <u>Inspect Documents</u>: This will check your document for hidden and other information. Once you click on this, a dialog box appears. Tick the item you intend to inspect and a summarized result will appear. Below is the sample of the report:

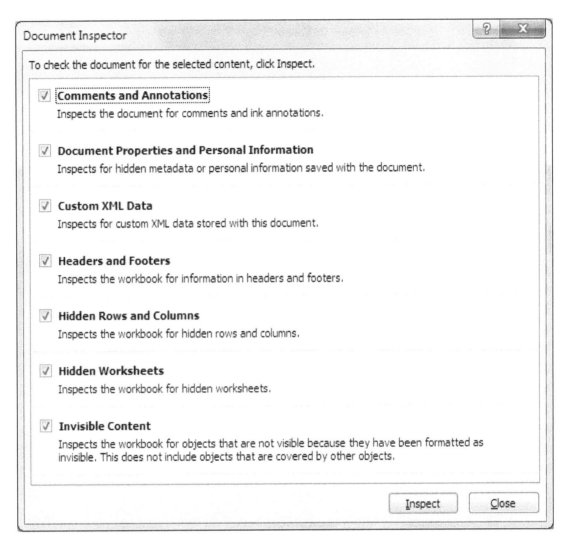

Fig 1.5

c) <u>Encrypt Document</u>: Enables you to increase the security features of your document by assigning a password. Once clicked, the dialog box below appears:

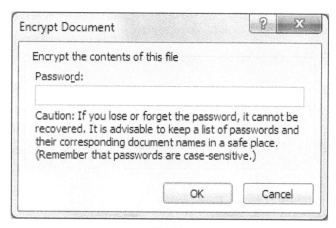

Fig 1.6

Type in the password and click OK. Confirm the password and save the document before exiting. If you want to open the document, you will be required to supply a password.

Warning: If you forget the password, you will not be able to open the file again.

d) <u>Restrict Permission</u>: This enables you to grant people access to your workbook with restricted permissions. If you are doing this for the first time, you must be connected to the internet in order to complete the process and you must have a Microsoft Live ID.

e) <u>Add Digital Signature</u>: You will only be able to use this option if you have a digital certificate. It enables you to be able to digitally sign Microsoft Office documents. You can get digital certificate from a third party vendor or create your own. Note however that others may not be able to verify your digital ID if you create your own digital certificate.

f) <u>Mark as Final</u>: This makes the workbook read only to all readers.

g) <u>Run Compatibility Checker</u>: Checks whether you have incompatible features in the file. Generally, Excel will check for compatibility features and warn you if there are issues when saving your file.

Send a File: This depend on what you installed. You can send your workbook to a Bluetooth device, email or Internet Fax

Publish a File: You can actually publish your file on the internet or electronically save the document for other people. This can be done in the following ways:

<u>Excel Services</u>: Saves your workbook for Excel Services which will enable you to specify what is shown in the browser. When you select this option, a dialog box appears where you will be required to type the name of your file. Check the box besides Open in Excel Services. Click on Excel Services Option to set other parameters and the following dialog box appears:

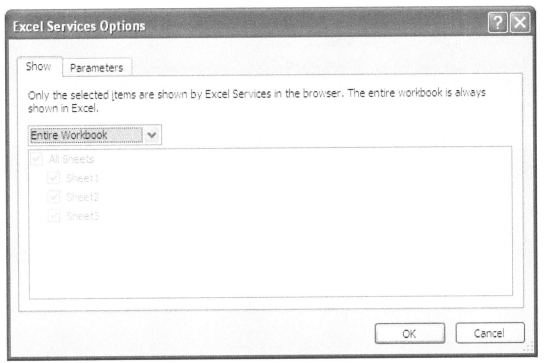

Fig 1.7

The Show tab on the dialog box displays all the worksheets. Use the arrow to select what you want viewers to view. The Parameters tab enables you to specify the editable cells in the worksheet.

Document Management Server: You can share your workbook by saving it to a document management server.

Create Document Workspace: Creates a new site for the workbook and keep the local copy synchronized.

Close: Closes the current file.

On the right hand corner (bottom) are two other short cuts:

Excel Options

For those that are familiar with Microsoft Excel, there are various options you can set. These options determine the behavior of Microsoft Excel. The earlier versions of Excel have these options under Tools. On the left side are the various option and the right hand shows the parameters you can set (see the diagram below). All of them have the default setting which will be sufficient for anybody using Microsoft Excel but some of the options will be discussed in case you need to make some changes:

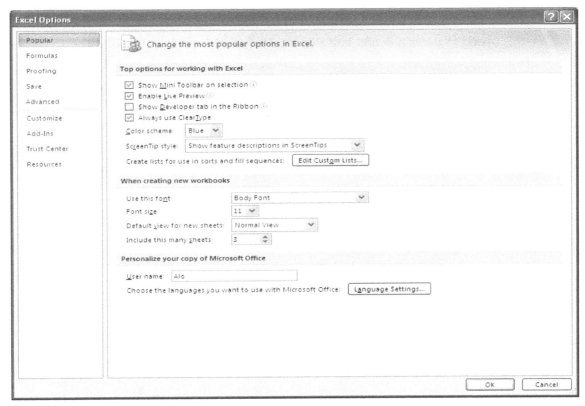

Fig 1.8

The following are the options:

1) **Popular:** This option enables you to set your Top options for working with Excel when creating new workbooks. It also enables you to personalize your copy of Excel. You can also set your language as well, but remember that some of the languages have limited support.

2) **Formula:** This relates to method of calculation and error handling. Under the Calculation options, you can select:

   a) Automatic: This option calculates all formula once a change is made. With this option, you can be rest assured that your worksheet will reflect the correct information at all times.

   b) Automatic except for data tables: This is similar to the automatic calculation mentioned above except that data tables will not be calculated. It means that if you forget to press function key F9, part of your worksheet can be misleading.

c) Manual: This will not calculate even if a major medication has taken place. You need to press function key F9 anytime you make a change and intend to see the effect of the changes made.

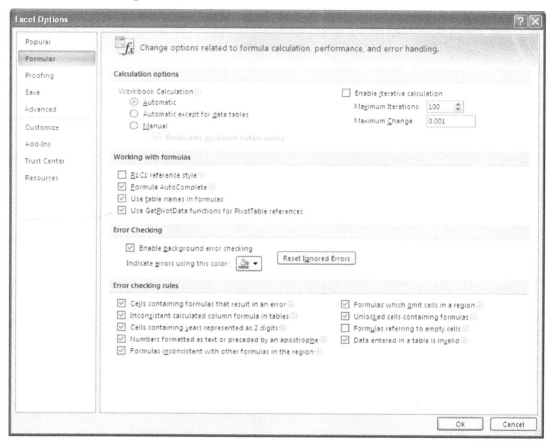

Fig 1.9

Under working with formulas, you can change your reference style to R1C1 in which case, Excel uses your relative position to create formula unlike the conventional method of using column labels and row numbers. Example: If you are in cell A3 and you type a formula =A1+A2. If R1C1 is not turned on, your formula will read =A1+A2 but if you turn on the R1C1 reference style, it reads: =+R[-1]C+R[-2]C. You can also enable Formula AutoComplete as well as other options.

You also have error checking and rule that you can set to show when an error is committed.

3) **Proofing**: This shows how Excel corrects and formats your text.

4) **Save:** Specifies how to save your file. You are allowed to set the following

   options:

   a. Save files in the Format: Determine your file format

   b. Set the time for auto recovery

   c. Set auto recovery file location

   d. Set default file location

There are so many other options you can set under Excel option.

Customize Quick Access Toolbar

Next to the Office Button is the Customize Quick Access Toolbar. The Toolbar is made up of short cut buttons such as New, Open, Save, E-mail, Quick Print, Print Preview, Spelling, Undo, Redo, Sort Ascending, Sort Descending, More Commands, etc. Once selected, it gives you quick access to such commands.

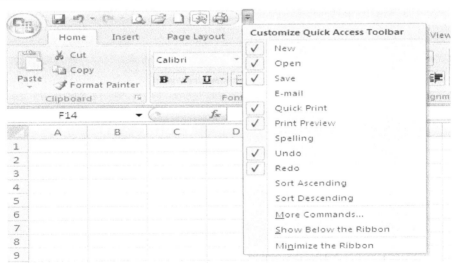

Fig 1.10

The Main Menu:

On the second row we have the standard or main menu (see Fig 1.1 above). Each menu has several icons under them. Following are the items under the main menu:

Home

Generally, most of the editing menu items are grouped under this heading. They include Font, Alignment, Formatting, Styles (all these will be discussed under Formatting your worksheet). Others include Clipboard (discussed under copy and paste) and Cells (discussed under Formatting Cells).

Insert

You can insert Tables (PivotTable, Table), Illustrations (Clip Art, Shapes, Smart Art and Fig), Charts, Links and Texts. Each of the items will be discussed later in the book.

Page Layout

Fully discussed under Printing your job

Formulas

We have various functions that can be inserted, mode of calculation, name definition and others.

Data

All data manipulation and related functions are grouped under this heading.

Review

Under Review, we have Proofing, protection and others

View

We have various worksheet views, Macro and other functions under View.

Add-Ins:

Under the Add-Ins, you will be able to use some customized tasks, user defined application or third party modules.

The Function

The Function enables you to insert formula from inbuilt functions. This could be financials, mathematical, etc. A dialog box appears once you click on the function (see Fig 1.11). The dialog box has three sections:

a) Search for a function: where you can type a brief description of what you want to do and then click Go.

b) Or select a category from a drop down list of functions

c) Select a function

Once you highlight a function, the syntax of the function selected will be displayed.

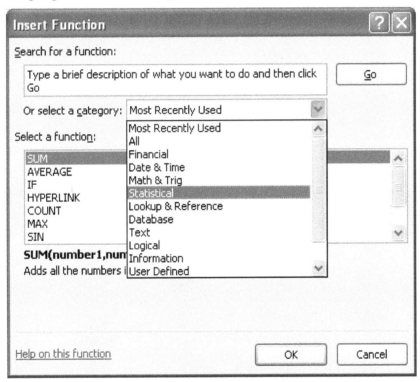

Fig 1.11

The Formula Bar

The Formula Bar displays the information entered in a cell at any point in time.

At the bottom end of each worksheet are left, right, arrows and the existing sheets. You can rename the sheet, delete them or copy from one sheet to another.

Notes:

2

General Terminologies

What is a Spreadsheet

Several Authors, Writers and Developers have defined Spreadsheet in various ways. Here are some of their definitions:

- "A computer application that displays multiple cells that together makes up a grid consisting of rows and columns, each cell containing either alphanumeric text or numeric values"

- "A spreadsheet, also known as a worksheet, contains rows and columns and is used to record and compare numerical or financial data"

- "A spreadsheet is a sheet of paper that shows accounting or other data in rows and columns"

- "A spreadsheet is also a computer application program that simulates a physical spreadsheet by capturing, displaying, and manipulating data arranged in rows and columns."

- "A spreadsheet is the computer equivalent of a paper ledger sheet. It consists of a grid made from columns and rows. It is an environment that can make number manipulation easy and somewhat painless"

Without going into too many technicalities, we will adopt the simplest of the definitions above that says "a spreadsheet is a sheet of paper that shows accounting or other information in rows and columns". Microsoft Excel is basically an electronic spreadsheet with inbuilt functions aimed at improving performance. With Microsoft Excel, you can automate repetitive task and perform complex calculations within seconds.

Workbook

A workbook is an Excel file containing one or more worksheets arranged in tabs. A workbook can contain as many worksheets as possible depending on the resources of your computer i.e. memory size. By default, a workbook contains 3 worksheets but you can insert additional worksheets as and when needed. Each workbook has 16 million colors and can be formatted with various fonts. A workbook must contain at least one visible worksheet.

Worksheet

A Worksheet on the other hand is a collection of cells arranged in rows and columns (see Fig 2.0 below). This is where your information is entered and manipulated. A worksheet can contain as many as 1,048,576 rows and 16,384 columns.

The rows could be numbered row 1, row 2, row 3, etc while the columns could be arranged either numerically 1,2,3,4, etc or alphabetically a, b, c, d, etc. The important thing worthy of note is that the arrangement makes the spreadsheet easy to reference.

Rows and Columns

Rows are arranged horizontally while the columns are arranged vertically. In the latest version of Excel, each row can be expanded up to 409 points while each column can have up to 255 characters. You can insert or delete Rows or columns at any time.

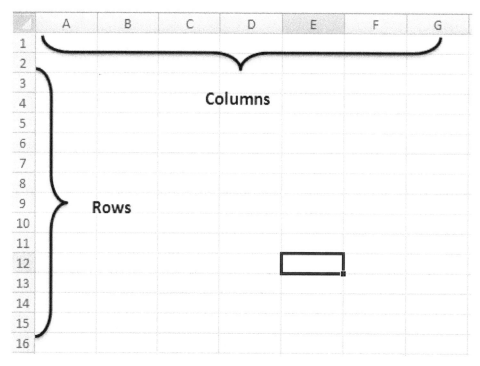

Fig 2.0

You can easily use terminology like I am in column A row 1 or my cursor is on column F row 5. The column is combined with the row for reference purposes e.g. A1, F5. This leads us to the next definition, "Cell"

Cell

Cell can be defined as a rectangular box or an intercession of a column and row. In the diagram (Fig 2.1) below, the shaded portion is a cell and can be identified as column B row 2 or simply put cell B2. A cell can contain information in form of numbers, alphabets or alpha-numeric and can as well be left blank. You can also expand both the row and the column of a cell. A cell can contain up to 32,767 characters

Range:

Another important term in Excel that you will be coming across from time to time is range. This is simply a cell or combination of cells. The portion highlighted above on Fig 2.1 is a range and can be referenced as E3 to G7

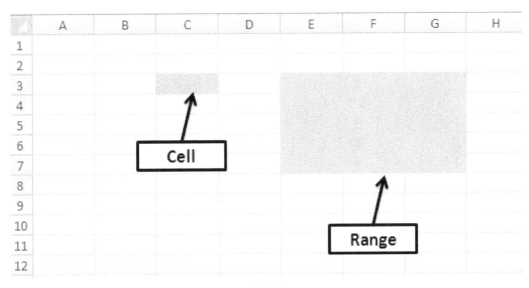

Fig 2.1

Referencing in Microsoft Excel

Cell reference in Microsoft Excel can be relative or absolute. If you have a formula in a cell and copy the formula to another cell, Excel will logically adjust the formula with reference to the original position of the first formula. For example, if you have formula adding cell A1 to cell B1 i.e. =(A1+B1) in cell C1 and copy the formula to cell C2, the formula will automatically change to =(A2+B2). This is what we referred to as relative reference. On the other hand, if the cell is made absolute, the reference will not change. This is simply done by inserting the $ sign before the column or row in the reference, e.g. $A1 simply means that no matter where you copy the formula, it will still refer to column A while rows will be changing. In this formula, column A has been made absolute. To make a row absolute, simply insert the Dollar sign $ before the row number. Using the above reference A1, we will make only the row absolute by typing A$1. We can make both the row and the column absolute as well by typing $A$2. Let's look at the following worksheet:

	A	B	C	D	E	F	G
			Total # of				Total # of
1	Orange	Apple	Fruits		Orange	Apple	Fruits
2	2	5			5	5	
3	6	4			10	15	
4	8	3			12	3	
5							

Fig 2.2

Type the formula =A2+B2 in Cell C2; =$A3+B3 in cell C3 and =$A4+$B4 in cell C4.

Highlight cell C2 to C5 and copy. Place your cursor in cell G2 and paste. Your screen will reflect the following:

	A	B	C	D	E	F	G	H
			Total # of				Total # of	
1	Orange	Apple	Fruits		Orange	Apple	Fruits	
2	2	5	7		5	5	10	
3	6	4	10		10	15	21	
4	8	3	11		12	3	11	
5								

Fig 2.3

You will notice the following answers: C2 gives you 7, C3 gives 10 and C4 gives 11. Remember you copied range C2:C4 to G2 and you have the following answers:

G2 = 10 because there was no absolute reference.

G3 = 21 because the original formula you copied from cell C3 made absolute reference to A and as a result, the formula in G3 reads $A3 + F3 = 6 + 15 = 21

G4 = 11 because the original formula you copied from cell C3 made absolute reference to column A and column B and as a result, the formula in G4 reads $A4 + $B4 = 8 + 3 = 11.

The same method is applicable to rows.

Circular Reference

Circular Reference is a situation where a formula directly or indirectly refers to itself. This can cause a major problem for your worksheet or even cause Excel to perform illegal operation. Circular reference will occur if you enter a formula that erroneously picks the cell that contains the formula. For example in fig 2.2 above, enter the formula =SUM(A2:A5) in cell A5. Circular reference will occur because your answer is expected to be in cell A5 and your formula included cell A5 in the formula.

Once there is circular reference, an error message appears on the status bar showing where the circular reference occurs:

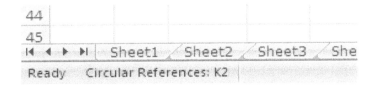

Fig 2.2

If you have more than one worksheet with circular references, you need to click each of the sheets and make necessary corrections. Once it is corrected, the circular reference error disappears.

3

Keyboard/ Shortcuts

You will cover:

- *The Function Keys*
- *Key Combinations*
- *Short Cut Keys*

Getting the job done is a function of what you know in Excel and the keyboard is a wonderful place to start learning shortcut. You can combine most of the keys to create shortcut in Excel that will facilitate your job and improve efficiency. Some of the keys you can combine with others are listed below:

Function Keys:

These are keys labeled F1 to F12

Key Combination	Function
F1	
F1	Help
Alt+F1	Create chart of current range. Note: • Highlight the range first before pressing Alt+F1. • One disadvantage of this is that the number of times you press these keys will determine the number of charts generated. In order not to reduce your system resources, press the combination only once.
Ctrl+F1	Display or hide the user interface i.e. the ribbon or buttons. This is also applicable to Microsoft Word.
Alt+Shift+F1	Insert a new worksheet

F2	
F2	Edit current cell
Shift+F2	Create or edit comment
Ctrl+F2	Print Preview

| Alt+F2 | Save as |

F3	
F3	Display or paste range names
Shift+F3	Insert function or formula
Ctrl+F3	Name manager

F4	
F4	Repeat last command if possible
Alt+F4	Close all opened workbook
Ctrl+F4	Close the selected workbook window
Shift+F4	Repeats the last search you made

F5	
F5	Go to dialog box
Ctrl+F5	Restore window
Shift+F5	Find & Replace dialog box

F6	
F6	This is particularly useful if for some reasons you don't have a mouse. It enables you to select various commands using the keyboard. It tags each of the command using alphabets and numbers which you can use to invoke your required command.
Shift+F6	Very similar to F6
Ctrl+F6	Move between opened workbooks

F7	
F7	Display Spelling dialog box

Ctrl+F7	Move active window if not maximized

F8	
F8	Turn extend mode on or off. With this, you can select range without using mouse or holding down your shift key
Shift+F8	Add non adjacent cell to your selection. This is similar to holding down Crtl + mouse buttons
Ctrl+F8	Sizing of window
Alt+F8	Display Macro dialog box

F9	
F9	Calculate the entire workbook
Shift+F9	Calculate only current worksheet
Ctrl+Alt+F9	Calculate all opened workbooks
Ctrl+Alt+Shift+F9	Calculate all opened workbooks
Ctrl+F9	Minimize a workbook to an icon

F10	
F10	Turns key tips on/off
Shift+F10	Short cut menu
Alt+Shift+F10	Menu for smart tag items
Ctrl+F10	Maximize or restore selected workbook window

F11	
F11	Same as Alt+F1 above
Shift+F11	Same as Alt+Shift+F1 above

Alt+F11	Run Visual Basic Editor
Ctrl+F11	Insert Macro worksheet

F12	
F12	Save as
Shift+F12	Automatically save your workbook with the last name
Ctrl+F12	Display Open dialog box

Ctrl+	applies or removes
1	Format Cell
2	Bold
3	Italic
4	Underline
5	Strikethrough
6	hide or displays objects
8	Displays or hides the outline symbols
9	Hide selected rows
0	Hide selected columns
A	Select Entire sheet
B	Bold
C	Copy
D	Fill down
F	Find
G	Goto
H	Find and replace
I	Italic
K	Hyperlink

N	New blank workbook
O	Open
P	Print
R	Fill right
S	Save
T	Create Table
U	Underline
V	Paste
W	Close workbook
X	Cut
Y	Repeat last command
Z	Undo

Ctrl + Shift +

(	Unhide row
)	Unhide column
&	Outline Border
_	Remove outline border
-	General number format
$	Currency format
%	Percentage format
^	Exponential format
#	Date format
@	Time format
!	Number format
*	current region
:	current time

"	copy value above
+	Insert
-	Delete
;	current date
'	display cell value or formula in the worksheet

Notes:

4

Basic Functions in Excel

You will cover:

- *Introduction*
- *Add-in and Automation functions*
- *Cube functions*
- *Database functions*
- *Date and time functions*
- *Engineering functions*
- *Financial functions*
- *Information functions*
- *Logical functions*
- *Lookup and reference functions*
- *Math and trigonometry functions*

Introduction

Microsoft Excel as a business application has so many mathematical functions that can help in accomplishing tasks. Ability to use the inbuilt formulas will be of a tremendous advantage to users. Some of them are complex while some are simple. We will consider some of the Excel formulas in this section.

In Microsoft Excel, you can type in your formula manually if you know the correct syntax or insert the formula using the **fx** function discussed on page 21.

The following are the categories of the Worksheet Functions:

Add-in and Automation functions

Cube functions

Database functions

Date and time functions

Engineering functions

Financial functions

Information functions

Logical functions

Lookup and reference functions

Math and trigonometry functions

Statistical functions

Text functions

They are so many that we will not be able to discuss them all but below are the functions reproduced from Microsoft Excel Help. I will make attempt to discuss very few of them.

Add-in and Automation functions

CALL   Calls a procedure in a dynamic link library or code resource

EUROCONVERT   Converts a number to euros, converts a number from euros to a euro member currency, or converts a number from one euro member currency to another by using the euro as an intermediary (triangulation)

GETPIVOTDATA   Returns data stored in a PivotTable report

REGISTER.ID   Returns the register ID of the specified dynamic link library (DLL) or code resource that has been previously registered

SQL.REQUEST   Connects with an external data source and runs a query from a worksheet, then returns the result as an array without the need for macro programming

Cube functions

CUBEKPIMEMBER   Returns a key performance indicator (KPI) name, property, and measure, and displays the name and property in the cell. A KPI is a quantifiable measurement, such as monthly gross profit or quarterly employee turnover, used to monitor an organization's performance.

CUBEMEMBER   Returns a member or tuple in a cube hierarchy. Use to validate that the member or tuple exists in the cube.

CUBEMEMBERPROPERTY   Returns the value of a member property in the cube. Use to validate that a member name exists within the cube and to return the specified property for this member.

CUBERANKEDMEMBER   Returns the nth, or ranked, member in a set. Use to return one or more elements in a set, such as the top sales performer or top 10 students.

CUBESET   Defines a calculated set of members or tuples by sending a set expression to the cube on the server, which creates the set, and then returns that set to Microsoft Office Excel.

| CUBESETCOUNT | Returns the number of items in a set. |
| CUBEVALUE | Returns an aggregated value from a cube. |

Database functions

DAVERAGE	Returns the average of selected database entries
DCOUNT	Counts the cells that contain numbers in a database
DCOUNTA	Counts nonblank cells in a database
DGET	Extracts from a database a single record that matches the specified criteria
DMAX	Returns the maximum value from selected database entries
DMIN	Returns the minimum value from selected database entries
DPRODUCT	Multiplies the values in a particular field of records that match the criteria in a database
DSTDEV	Estimates the standard deviation based on a sample of selected database entries
DSTDEVP	Calculates the standard deviation based on the entire population of selected database entries
DSUM	Adds the numbers in the field column of records in the database that match the criteria
DVAR	Estimates variance based on a sample from selected database entries
DVARP	Calculates variance based on the entire population of selected database entries

Date and time functions

DATE	Returns the serial number of a particular date
DATEVALUE	Converts a date in the form of text to a serial number
DAY	Converts a serial number to a day of the month

DAYS360	Calculates the number of days between two dates based on a 360-day year
EDATE	Returns the serial number of the date that is the indicated number of months before or after the start date
EOMONTH	Returns the serial number of the last day of the month before or after a specified number of months
HOUR	Converts a serial number to an hour
MINUTE	Converts a serial number to a minute
MONTH	Converts a serial number to a month
NETWORKDAYS	Returns the number of whole workdays between two dates
NOW	Returns the serial number of the current date and time
SECOND	Converts a serial number to a second
TIME	Returns the serial number of a particular time
TIMEVALUE	Converts a time in the form of text to a serial number
TODAY	Returns the serial number of today's date
WEEKDAY	Converts a serial number to a day of the week
WEEKNUM	Converts a serial number to a number representing where the week falls numerically with a year
WORKDAY	Returns the serial number of the date before or after a specified number of workdays
YEAR	Converts a serial number to a year
YEARFRAC	Returns the year fraction representing the number of whole days between start_date and end_date

Engineering functions

Function	Description
BESSELI	Returns the modified Bessel function In(x)
BESSELJ	Returns the Bessel function Jn(x)

BESSELK	Returns the modified Bessel function $K_n(x)$
BESSELY	Returns the Bessel function $Y_n(x)$
BIN2DEC	Converts a binary number to decimal
BIN2HEX	Converts a binary number to hexadecimal
BIN2OCT	Converts a binary number to octal
COMPLEX	Converts real and imaginary coefficients into a complex number
CONVERT	Converts a number from one measurement system to another
DEC2BIN	Converts a decimal number to binary
DEC2HEX	Converts a decimal number to hexadecimal
DEC2OCT	Converts a decimal number to octal
DELTA	Tests whether two values are equal
ERF	Returns the error function
ERFC	Returns the complementary error function
GESTEP	Tests whether a number is greater than a threshold value
HEX2BIN	Converts a hexadecimal number to binary
HEX2DEC	Converts a hexadecimal number to decimal
HEX2OCT	Converts a hexadecimal number to octal
IMABS	Returns the absolute value (modulus) of a complex number
IMAGINARY	Returns the imaginary coefficient of a complex number
IMARGUMENT	Returns the argument theta, an angle expressed in radians
IMCONJUGATE	Returns the complex conjugate of a complex number
IMCOS	Returns the cosine of a complex number
IMDIV	Returns the quotient of two complex numbers
IMEXP	Returns the exponential of a complex number
IMLN	Returns the natural logarithm of a complex number
IMLOG10	Returns the base-10 logarithm of a complex number
IMLOG2	Returns the base-2 logarithm of a complex number
IMPOWER	Returns a complex number raised to an integer power

IMPRODUCT	Returns the product of complex numbers
IMREAL	Returns the real coefficient of a complex number
IMSIN	Returns the sine of a complex number
IMSQRT	Returns the square root of a complex number
IMSUB	Returns the difference between two complex numbers
IMSUM	Returns the sum of complex numbers
OCT2BIN	Converts an octal number to binary
OCT2DEC	Converts an octal number to decimal
OCT2HEX	Converts an octal number to hexadecimal

Financial functions

ACCRINT	Returns the accrued interest for a security that pays periodic interest
ACCRINTM	Returns the accrued interest for a security that pays interest at maturity
AMORDEGRC	Returns the depreciation for each accounting period by using a depreciation coefficient
AMORLINC	Returns the depreciation for each accounting period
COUPDAYBS	Returns the number of days from the beginning of the coupon period to the settlement date
COUPDAYS	Returns the number of days in the coupon period that contains the settlement date
COUPDAYSNC	Returns the number of days from the settlement date to the next coupon date
COUPNCD	Returns the next coupon date after the settlement date
COUPNUM	Returns the number of coupons payable between the settlement date and maturity date
COUPPCD	Returns the previous coupon date before the settlement date
CUMIPMT	Returns the cumulative interest paid between two periods

CUMPRINC	Returns the cumulative principal paid on a loan between two periods
DB	Returns the depreciation of an asset for a specified period by using the fixed-declining balance method
DDB	Returns the depreciation of an asset for a specified period by using the double-declining balance method or some other method that you specify
DISC	Returns the discount rate for a security
DOLLARDE	Converts a dollar price, expressed as a fraction, into a dollar price, expressed as a decimal number
DOLLARFR	Converts a dollar price, expressed as a decimal number, into a dollar price, expressed as a fraction
DURATION	Returns the annual duration of a security with periodic interest payments
EFFECT	Returns the effective annual interest rate
FV	Returns the future value of an investment
FVSCHEDULE	Returns the future value of an initial principal after applying a series of compound interest rates
INTRATE	Returns the interest rate for a fully invested security
IPMT	Returns the interest payment for an investment for a given period
IRR	Returns the internal rate of return for a series of cash flows
ISPMT	Calculates the interest paid during a specific period of an investment
MDURATION	Returns the Macauley modified duration for a security with an assumed par value of $100
MIRR	Returns the internal rate of return where positive and negative cash flows are financed at different rates
NOMINAL	Returns the annual nominal interest rate
NPER	Returns the number of periods for an investment
NPV	Returns the net present value of an investment based on a series of

periodic cash flows and a discount rate

ODDFPRICE   Returns the price per $100 face value of a security with an odd first period

ODDFYIELD   Returns the yield of a security with an odd first period

ODDLPRICE   Returns the price per $100 face value of a security with an odd last period

ODDLYIELD   Returns the yield of a security with an odd last period

PMT   Returns the periodic payment for an annuity

PPMT   Returns the payment on the principal for an investment for a given period

PRICE   Returns the price per $100 face value of a security that pays periodic interest

PRICEDISC   Returns the price per $100 face value of a discounted security

PRICEMAT   Returns the price per $100 face value of a security that pays interest at maturity

PV   Returns the present value of an investment

RATE   Returns the interest rate per period of an annuity

RECEIVED   Returns the amount received at maturity for a fully invested security

SLN   Returns the straight-line depreciation of an asset for one period

SYD   Returns the sum-of-years' digits depreciation of an asset for a specified period

TBILLEQ   Returns the bond-equivalent yield for a Treasury bill

TBILLPRICE   Returns the price per $100 face value for a Treasury bill

TBILLYIELD   Returns the yield for a Treasury bill

VDB   Returns the depreciation of an asset for a specified or partial period by using a declining balance method

XIRR   Returns the internal rate of return for a schedule of cash flows that is not necessarily periodic

XNPV	Returns the net present value for a schedule of cash flows that is not necessarily periodic
YIELD	Returns the yield on a security that pays periodic interest
YIELDDISC	Returns the annual yield for a discounted security; for example, a Treasury bill
YIELDMAT	Returns the annual yield of a security that pays interest at maturity

Information functions

CELL	Returns information about the formatting, location, or contents of a cell
ERROR.TYPE	Returns a number corresponding to an error type
INFO	Returns information about the current operating environment
ISBLANK	Returns TRUE if the value is blank
ISERR	Returns TRUE if the value is any error value except #N/A
ISERROR	Returns TRUE if the value is any error value
ISEVEN	Returns TRUE if the number is even
ISLOGICAL	Returns TRUE if the value is a logical value
ISNA	Returns TRUE if the value is the #N/A error value
ISNONTEXT	Returns TRUE if the value is not text
ISNUMBER	Returns TRUE if the value is a number
ISODD	Returns TRUE if the number is odd
ISREF	Returns TRUE if the value is a reference
ISTEXT	Returns TRUE if the value is text
N	Returns a value converted to a number
NA	Returns the error value #N/A
TYPE	Returns a number indicating the data type of a value

Logical functions

AND	Returns TRUE if all of its arguments are TRUE
FALSE	Returns the logical value FALSE
IF	Specifies a logical test to perform
IFERROR	Returns a value you specify if a formula evaluates to an error; otherwise, returns the result of the formula
NOT	Reverses the logic of its argument

OR	Returns TRUE if any argument is TRUE
TRUE	Returns the logical value TRUE

Lookup and reference functions

ADDRESS	Returns a reference as text to a single cell in a worksheet
AREAS	Returns the number of areas in a reference
CHOOSE	Chooses a value from a list of values
COLUMN	Returns the column number of a reference
COLUMNS	Returns the number of columns in a reference
HLOOKUP	Looks in the top row of an array and returns the value of the indicated cell
HYPERLINK	Creates a shortcut or jump that opens a document stored on a network server, an intranet, or the Internet
INDEX	Uses an index to choose a value from a reference or array
INDIRECT	Returns a reference indicated by a text value
LOOKUP	Looks up values in a vector or array
MATCH	Looks up values in a reference or array
OFFSET	Returns a reference offset from a given reference
ROW	Returns the row number of a reference
ROWS	Returns the number of rows in a reference
RTD	Retrieves real-time data from a program that supports COM automation (Automation: A way to work with an application's objects from another application or development tool. Formerly called OLE Automation, Automation is an industry standard and a feature of the Component Object Model (COM).)
TRANSPOSE	Returns the transpose of an array
VLOOKUP	Looks in the first column of an array and moves across the row to return

the value of a cell

Math and trigonometry functions

ABS	Returns the absolute value of a number
ACOS	Returns the arccosine of a number
ACOSH	Returns the inverse hyperbolic cosine of a number
ASIN	Returns the arcsine of a number
ASINH	Returns the inverse hyperbolic sine of a number
ATAN	Returns the arctangent of a number
ATAN2	Returns the arctangent from x- and y-coordinates
ATANH	Returns the inverse hyperbolic tangent of a number
CEILING	Rounds a number to the nearest integer or to the nearest multiple of significance
COMBIN	Returns the number of combinations for a given number of objects
COS	Returns the cosine of a number
COSH	Returns the hyperbolic cosine of a number
DEGREES	Converts radians to degrees
EVEN	Rounds a number up to the nearest even integer
EXP	Returns e raised to the power of a given number
FACT	Returns the factorial of a number
FACTDOUBLE	Returns the double factorial of a number
FLOOR	Rounds a number down, toward zero
GCD	Returns the greatest common divisor
INT	Rounds a number down to the nearest integer
LCM	Returns the least common multiple
LN	Returns the natural logarithm of a number
LOG	Returns the logarithm of a number to a specified base
LOG10	Returns the base-10 logarithm of a number

MDETERM	Returns the matrix determinant of an array
MINVERSE	Returns the matrix inverse of an array
MMULT	Returns the matrix product of two arrays
MOD	Returns the remainder from division
MROUND	Returns a number rounded to the desired multiple
MULTINOMIAL	Returns the multinomial of a set of numbers
ODD	Rounds a number up to the nearest odd integer
PI	Returns the value of pi
POWER	Returns the result of a number raised to a power
PRODUCT	Multiplies its arguments
QUOTIENT	Returns the integer portion of a division
RADIANS	Converts degrees to radians
RAND	Returns a random number between 0 and 1
RANDBETWEEN	Returns a random number between the numbers you specify
ROMAN	Converts an arabic numeral to roman, as text
ROUND	Rounds a number to a specified number of digits
ROUNDDOWN	Rounds a number down, toward zero
ROUNDUP	Rounds a number up, away from zero
SERIESSUM	Returns the sum of a power series based on the formula
SIGN	Returns the sign of a number
SIN	Returns the sine of the given angle
SINH	Returns the hyperbolic sine of a number
SQRT	Returns a positive square root
SQRTPI	Returns the square root of (number * pi)
SUBTOTAL	Returns a subtotal in a list or database
SUM	Adds its arguments
SUMIF	Adds the cells specified by a given criteria
SUMIFS	Adds the cells in a range that meet multiple criteria

SUMPRODUCT	Returns the sum of the products of corresponding array components
SUMSQ	Returns the sum of the squares of the arguments
SUMX2MY2	Returns the sum of the difference of squares of corresponding values in two arrays
SUMX2PY2	Returns the sum of the sum of squares of corresponding values in two arrays
SUMXMY2	Returns the sum of squares of differences of corresponding values in two arrays
TAN	Returns the tangent of a number
TANH	Returns the hyperbolic tangent of a number
TRUNC	Truncates a number to an integer

Statistical functions

Function	Description
AVEDEV	Returns the average of the absolute deviations of data points from their mean
AVERAGE	Returns the average of its arguments
AVERAGEA	Returns the average of its arguments, including numbers, text, and logical values
AVERAGEIF	Returns the average (arithmetic mean) of all the cells in a range that meet a given criteria
AVERAGEIFS	Returns the average (arithmetic mean) of all cells that meet multiple criteria.
BETADIST	Returns the beta cumulative distribution function
BETAINV	Returns the inverse of the cumulative distribution function for a specified beta distribution
BINOMDIST	Returns the individual term binomial distribution probability
CHIDIST	Returns the one-tailed probability of the chi-squared distribution

CHIINV	Returns the inverse of the one-tailed probability of the chi-squared distribution
CHITEST	Returns the test for independence
CONFIDENCE	Returns the confidence interval for a population mean
CORREL	Returns the correlation coefficient between two data sets
COUNT	Counts how many numbers are in the list of arguments
COUNTA	Counts how many values are in the list of arguments
COUNTBLANK	Counts the number of blank cells within a range
COUNTIF	Counts the number of cells within a range that meet the given criteria
COUNTIFS	Counts the number of cells within a range that meet multiple criteria
COVAR	Returns covariance, the average of the products of paired deviations
CRITBINOM	Returns the smallest value for which the cumulative binomial distribution is less than or equal to a criterion value
DEVSQ	Returns the sum of squares of deviations
EXPONDIST	Returns the exponential distribution
FDIST	Returns the F probability distribution
FINV	Returns the inverse of the F probability distribution
FISHER	Returns the Fisher transformation
FISHERINV	Returns the inverse of the Fisher transformation
FORECAST	Returns a value along a linear trend
FREQUENCY	Returns a frequency distribution as a vertical array
FTEST	Returns the result of an F-test
GAMMADIST	Returns the gamma distribution
GAMMAINV	Returns the inverse of the gamma cumulative distribution
GAMMALN	Returns the natural logarithm of the gamma function, $\Gamma(x)$
GEOMEAN	Returns the geometric mean
GROWTH	Returns values along an exponential trend

HARMEAN	Returns the harmonic mean
HYPGEOMDIST	Returns the hypergeometric distribution
INTERCEPT	Returns the intercept of the linear regression line
KURT	Returns the kurtosis of a data set
LARGE	Returns the k-th largest value in a data set
LINEST	Returns the parameters of a linear trend
LOGEST	Returns the parameters of an exponential trend
LOGINV	Returns the inverse of the lognormal distribution
LOGNORMDIST	Returns the cumulative lognormal distribution
MAX	Returns the maximum value in a list of arguments
MAXA	Returns the maximum value in a list of arguments, including numbers, text, and logical values
MEDIAN	Returns the median of the given numbers
MIN	Returns the minimum value in a list of arguments
MINA	Returns the smallest value in a list of arguments, including numbers, text, and logical values
MODE	Returns the most common value in a data set
NEGBINOMDIST	Returns the negative binomial distribution
NORMDIST	Returns the normal cumulative distribution
NORMINV	Returns the inverse of the normal cumulative distribution
NORMSDIST	Returns the standard normal cumulative distribution
NORMSINV	Returns the inverse of the standard normal cumulative distribution
PEARSON	Returns the Pearson product moment correlation coefficient
PERCENTILE	Returns the k-th percentile of values in a range
PERCENTRANK	Returns the percentage rank of a value in a data set
PERMUT	Returns the number of permutations for a given number of objects
POISSON	Returns the Poisson distribution
PROB	Returns the probability that values in a range are between two limits

QUARTILE	Returns the quartile of a data set
RANK	Returns the rank of a number in a list of numbers
RSQ	Returns the square of the Pearson product moment correlation coefficient
SKEW	Returns the skewness of a distribution
SLOPE	Returns the slope of the linear regression line
SMALL	Returns the k-th smallest value in a data set
STANDARDIZE	Returns a normalized value
STDEV	Estimates standard deviation based on a sample
STDEVA	Estimates standard deviation based on a sample, including numbers, text, and logical values
STDEVP	Calculates standard deviation based on the entire population
STDEVPA	Calculates standard deviation based on the entire population, including numbers, text, and logical values
STEYX	Returns the standard error of the predicted y-value for each x in the regression
TDIST	Returns the Student's t-distribution
TINV	Returns the inverse of the Student's t-distribution
TREND	Returns values along a linear trend
TRIMMEAN	Returns the mean of the interior of a data set
TTEST	Returns the probability associated with a Student's t-test
VAR	Estimates variance based on a sample
VARA	Estimates variance based on a sample, including numbers, text, and logical values
VARP	Calculates variance based on the entire population
VARPA	Calculates variance based on the entire population, including numbers, text, and logical values
WEIBULL	Returns the Weibull distribution

| ZTEST | Returns the one-tailed probability-value of a z-test |

Text functions

ASC	Changes full-width (double-byte) English letters or katakana within a character string to half-width (single-byte) characters
BAHTTEXT	Converts a number to text, using the ß (baht) currency format
CHAR	Returns the character specified by the code number
CLEAN	Removes all nonprintable characters from text
CODE	Returns a numeric code for the first character in a text string
CONCATENATE	Joins several text items into one text item
DOLLAR	Converts a number to text, using the $ (dollar) currency format
EXACT	Checks to see if two text values are identical
FIND, FINDB	Finds one text value within another (case-sensitive)
FIXED	Formats a number as text with a fixed number of decimals
JIS	Changes half-width (single-byte) English letters or katakana within a character string to full-width (double-byte) characters
LEFT, LEFTB	Returns the leftmost characters from a text value
LEN, LENB	Returns the number of characters in a text string
LOWER	Converts text to lowercase
MID, MIDB	Returns a specific number of characters from a text string starting at the position you specify
PHONETIC	Extracts the phonetic (furigana) characters from a text string
PROPER	Capitalizes the first letter in each word of a text value
REPLACE, REPLACEB	Replaces characters within text
REPT	Repeats text a given number of times
RIGHT, RIGHTB	Returns the rightmost characters from a text value
SEARCH, SEARCHB	Finds one text value within another (not case-sensitive)

SUBSTITUTE	Substitutes new text for old text in a text string
T	Converts its arguments to text
TEXT	Formats a number and converts it to text
TRIM	Removes spaces from text
UPPER	Converts text to uppercase
VALUE	Converts a text argument to a number

Sum

This sums up your figures or generates the total of selected cells. The beauty of the Sum function is that you can combine it with several conditions such as if, ifs, etc.

Syntax: =sum(number1,number2,…) or =sum(A1:B5)

Let's add the following numbers together (1, 3,5,4,7,8,10)

You can add them by typing: =1+3+5+4+7+8+10

Or using =sum(1,3,5,4,7,8,10)

You can as well type the numbers in cells :

	A
1	1
2	3
3	5
4	4
5	7
6	8
7	10
8	38

Formula in cell a8: =SUM(A1:A8)

You can also achieve the above by simply clicking on the Σ AutoSum located on the Editing Menu which is under the Home from the Standard or Main Menu. This automatically sums up the range or numbers highlighted.

The above is the simplest form of the Sum function. How do we sum noncontiguous range? Let's take a look at the worksheet below:

	A	B
1	Name	Scores
2	John	50
3	James	60
4	Jack	40
5	Bull	75
6	John	40
7	James	30
8	Lol	20
9	Bull	70
10	Mem	50
11	Kim	45
12	Duck	35
13	Sam	30
14	Jayne	20

Fig 4.0

You can get the total of the above worksheet by clicking on the Auto Sum mentioned above or by simply type the formula =SUM(B2:B14) in cell A15.

How about finding the total of only the highlighted rows? Auto-Sum will not be able to achieve that and we need formula like:

=SUM(B2:B4,B7:B9,B11:B14)

Most users of Excel hardly use the above formula, rather they use formula like: =SUM(B2:B4)+SUM(B7:B9)+SUM(B11:B14). This is a longer process and the first is faster and simpler.

SUMIF

This is another beautiful tool when you are working on data with repeated information and you need to get the total of each item. In the above example, we have repeated names like James, Bull, John, etc. If you are to get the total scores of James and John, how do you get the answer? Some will use the formula =B3+B7 for James and =B2+B6 for John.

Imaging how difficult it will be if you are to do this for over 500 pupils with scores scattered over thousands of rows or columns.

SUMIF will achieve the result faster and better in such situation. Let's review the syntax of SUMIF:

Range: The range of cells you want to sum. Remember the range must be arranged in such a way that your criteria must be the first column in the range. In this example, your range will be A2:B14

=SUMIF(range,criteria,sum_range)

Criteria: The basis of arriving at your answer. In this example, John or James (range: A17:A18)

Sum_Range: The range containing the numbers you want to sum (range B2:B14)

Fig 4.1

Let's use SUMIF to accomplish the above. Do the following:

a) Type John in cell A17 and James in cell A18

b) Type =SUMIF(A2:B14,A17,B2:B14) in cell B17 and type the same formula in cell B18.

Compare your answers with the one you got manually.

Let's find the total of all numbers greater or equal to 45 by simply typing:

=SUMIF(B2:B14,">=45",B2:B14)

That formula gives you 350

Let's find the total of all numbers less or equal to 44 by simply typing:

=SUMIF(B2:B14,"<=44",B2:B14)

That formula gives you 215

Take a look at the data below. It contains the quantity of items sold in a particular region by Sales Agents. You may be requested to calculate the total sales of particular product either by an individual agent in a particular region. The SUM combined with the IF functions will be of tremendous help in this situation. Below is the syntax:

SUM(IF((range=x)*(range=y)*(range=z),range to sum))

From the table below, total computer sold in Lagos by James is 90.

	A	B	C	D
1	Name	Region	Product	Sales
2	John	Kano	Computer	50
3	James	Lagos	Computer	60
4	Jack	Jos	Computer	40
5	Bull	Enugu	Computer	75
6	John	Lagos	Computer	40
7	James	Lagos	Printer	30
8	Lol	Lagos	Computer	20
9	Bull	Kano	Printer	70
10	Mem	Jos	Printer	50
11	Kim	Kano	Printer	45
12	Duck	Kano	Computer	35
13	James	Lagos	Computer	30
14	Jayne	Lagos	Printer	20

Fig 4.2

To calculate this, type the formula as follows:

=SUM(IF((A2:A14="James")*(B2:B14="Lagos")*(C2:C14="Computer"),D2:D14))

If you press Enter to complete the formula, you will get an error message. This is because the formula is one of the array formulas (i.e. a formula that performs multiple calculations on one or more sets of values, and then returns either a single result or multiple results. Array formulas are enclosed between braces { } and are entered by pressing CTRL+SHIFT+ENTER.).

Press CTRL+SHIFT+ENTER and the formula will be changed as follows:

{=SUM(IF((A2:A14="James")*(B2:B14="Lagos")*(C2:C14="Computer),D2:D14))}

Also take note of the fact that the formula we used is not the conventional SUMIF earlier discussed.

SUMIFS

SUMIFS enables you to sum a particular range base on many criteria. It is one of the normal formulas similar to sum. The syntax is;

=SUMIFS(sum_range,criteria_range1,criteria1,criteria_range2,criteria1,etc)

Let's analyze the formula:

Sum_range is the range containing the figures you want to sum up

Criteria_Range1 is the range containing your first criterion (in the above example range A2 to A14 i.e. names of sales agents).

Criteria1 is the value you are looking for in the Criteria_Range1. From the above example, this will be James

Criteria_Range2 is the range containing your second criterion (in the above example range B2 to B14 i.e. Region).

Criteria2 is the value you are looking for in the Criteria_Range2. From the above example, this will be Lagos

Criteria_Range3 is the range containing your third criterion (in the above example range C2 to C14 i.e. Product).

Criteria3 is the value you are looking for in the Criteria_Range3. From the above example, this will be Computer.

To calculate the total computer sold by James in Lagos, type the following:

=SUMIFS(D2:D14,A2:A14,"James",B2:B14,"Lagos",C2:C14,"Computer")

The above gives you 90

5

Working

with Files

Introduction

We have discussed about functions, toolbars and other parts of Excel. We will now discuss how to create, modify and work with a simple worksheet.

Creating a Workbook

There are two ways to create a worksheet in Microsoft Excel as earlier mentioned. First is through the Office Button and the other through the Customized Quick Access Toolbar.

To create a workbook, follow the steps below:

a) Click the Office button and select New. A new workbook dialog box appears:

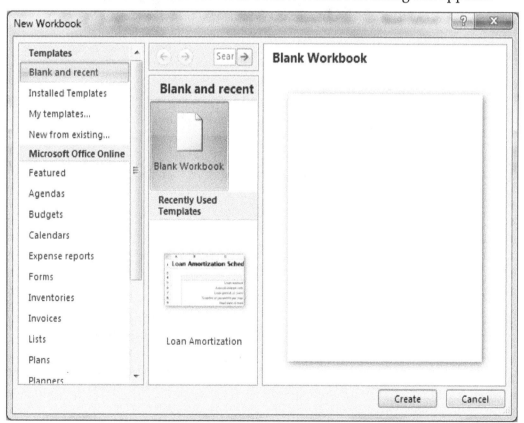

Fig 5.0

On the left hand side of the dialog box is a list of various Microsoft Excel in-built Templates that you can select from. Once selected, Excel will create a prototype of the template selected for you to modify and save.

Next is where you can type in Keyword for Excel to search Microsoft online for a template matching your search criteria. Click on the arrow besides the textbox to start the search.

Below the search bar is a blank workbook that you can used if you prefer starting your own workbook from the scratch.

Below the blank workbook are recently used templates

On the right is the preview of the templates. The preview enables you to see how your workbook will appear once created.

The Create or Cancel buttons will confirm or cancel your choice.

b) Highlight your template and click Create to confirm.

Let's create a Workbook that will calculate monthly repayment of loan. To do this, click on office button as discussed above and select New. From the New Workbook dialog box, select Loan Amortization and click Create. Your workbook will look like:

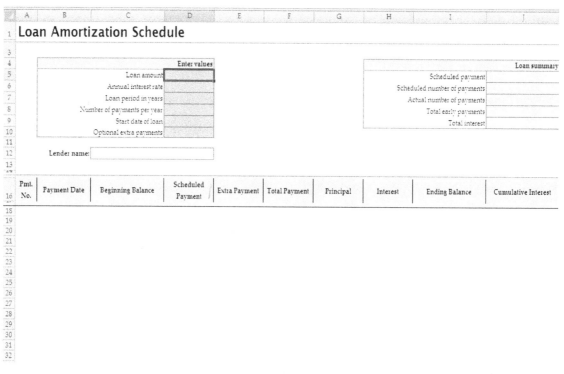

Fig 5.1

The workbook is duly protected as you can only fill the colored cells. Once you have filled in the Loan Amount, Annual Interest Rate, Loan period in year, Number of Payments, Start of the Loan and Optional Payment, Excel completes the repayment schedule.

Please note that creating a workbook through the Office Button gives you more options than using the Customized Access Tool Bar discussed below.

Using Customized Access Tool Bar

Creating Workbook using the Customized Access Tool Bar gives you only one option which is the Blank Workbook. Generally, the workbook comes with three worksheets but you can add as many worksheets as required. To create a workbook using the Customized Access Tool Bar, do the following:

- Click ⬚ (New File) from the Customized Quick Access Tool Bar and a new workbook will be created.

Opening an Existing File

You can open an existing workbook either from the Office Button or Customized Quick Access Tool Bar. Simply click on ⬚ either from the Office Button or Customized Quick Access Tool Bar. A dialog box appears with the directories from your computer.

Select the file you want to open.

Opening a Text File:

To open a text file in Microsoft Excel, do the following:

Click on ⬚ to open the file and a dialog box appears.

- If you know the name of the file, type the name of the file and click open.
- If you don't know the name of the file, select all files from the file extension and select the file.
- Click Open and a Text Import Dialog Box appears (see fig 5.2)

  The dialog box gives you the opportunity to select the original data type which can either be Delimited or Fixed Width.

  Delimited: Special character separate each field. This character could be comma, semi-colon, etc

  Fixed Width: Each field has a specified width

  Start Import at Row: Indicate the row where you want your data import to start e.g. do you want to start from row 1 or from row 5, etc.

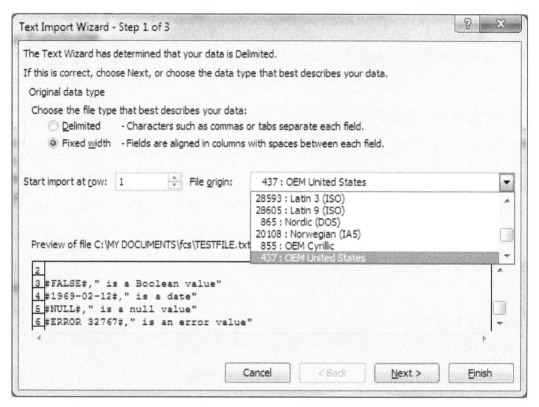

Fig 5.2

- Click Next and Text Import Wizard (Step 2 of 3) appears. This screen depends on your selection from the earlier screen. If you have chosen Delimited data type, the next screen appears:

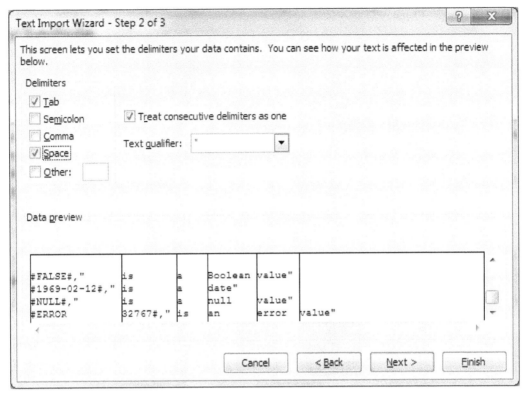

Fig 5.3

- From the above picture, we have selected characters that separate each field. You can combine those characters.

- If you have selected fixed width, your screen will be different from the above. You will be able to cut the data at your required positions (see fig 5.4).

  Simply click wherever you want to start a new column and the system automatically creates a vertical line on the spot

- Click on Next to go to Step 3 of 3

  Under step 3 of 3, you will be able to select the format for each column. Following are some of the available formats;

  o General format

  o Text

o Date

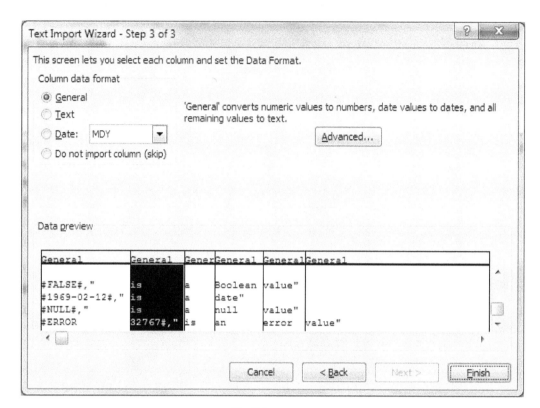

Fig 5.4

It is very important to set the format for each column if you are going to get the best result. For instance, if you have columns with 0001 and you did not format the column as text, it will be converted to 1 as the system will automatically format it as number. If you are formatting date, make sure you select the correct date system to avoid getting misleading information. For example, if you use American Date System for a file with British Date, your information will be distorted because 10/05/2009 means 10th May, 2009 in British and 5th October, 2009 in American system. If you are able to select the correct date format, you will be in good shape.

Simply highlight each column and select the format for the column until you have formatted all the columns.

- o You can also skip the particular column from being imported.

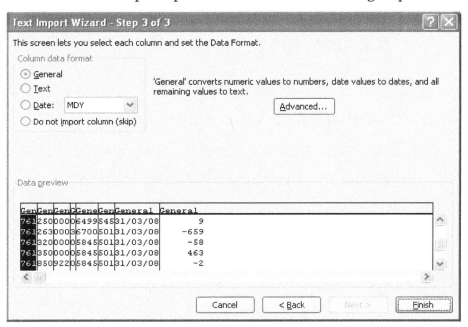

Fig 5.5

Click on the Advanced to set Decimal separator or thousand separator

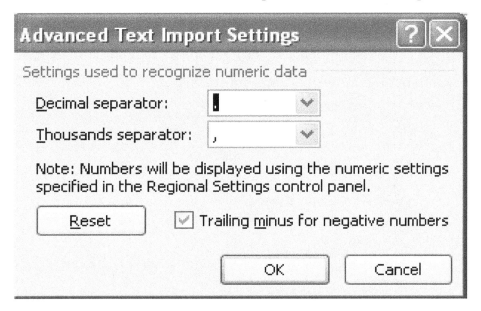

Fig 5.6

To close the Advanced Text Import Settings, click OK.

- Click on Finish to complete the import

- Review the file and if for any reason, the file is not retrieved properly, simply close the file and open it again.

Inserting/Deleting Rows, Columns and Sheets

Generally, when working with data, it is quite possible to omit a line or lines i.e. jump lines, Excel has made provision for you to be able to insert row or rows in-between lines. Same thing is applicable to columns. You might even need a new worksheet. Inserting rows, columns or sheets is a very simple process in Excel. There are two ways of inserting rows or columns. One is by clicking the right button of the mouse or by selecting Insert located under Home from the main menu.

To insert a row or column using the right button on the mouse, place your cursor on the row number or the column and click the right button, select insert and a blank row or column is inserted.

To delete a row or column using the right button on the mouse, place your cursor on the row number or the column and click the right button, select delete and the row goes off. The Insert Icon is located under Home from main menu:

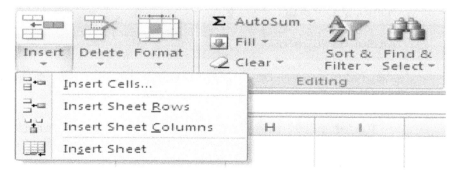

Fig 5.7

If you click the icon without touching the arrow below it, Excel shifts cells downward by the number of rows in the highlighted cells. Clicking the arrow rather than the icon gives you more options such as Insert Cells, Insert Sheet Rows, Insert Sheet Columns and Insert Sheet.

The Delete Icon is located under Home from main menu:

Fig 5.8

If you click the icon without touching the arrow below it, Excel shifts cells upward by the number of rows in the highlighted cells. Clicking the arrow rather than the icon gives you more options such as Delete Cells, Delete Sheet Rows, Delete Sheet Columns and Delete Sheet.

Formatting Workbook

This has been fully covered under Formatting Cells.

Workbook View

There are about five different views of a workbook as shown below:

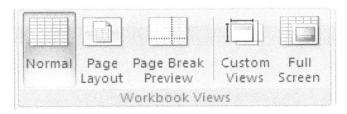

Fig 5.9

- **Normal View:** Display the entire worksheet

- **Page Layout:** Display the entire worksheet in pages depending on your page setup (landscape or portrait)

- **Page Break Preview:** Show where page breaks will be applied. You will also be able to insert or delete page breaks.

- **Custom Views:** Allow you to set the parameters for your desired view

- **Full Screen:** Remove both the Ribbon and the Main Menu

Headings/Gridlines

You can hide or show the Ruler, Gridlines, Formula Bar as well as Headings

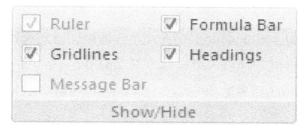

Fig 5.10

Gridlines: When this box is unchecked, the gridlines will disappear.

Headings: Uncheck this box to remove both the row numbers and the column labels.

Formula Bar: Check or unchecked this box to display or hide the formula bar.

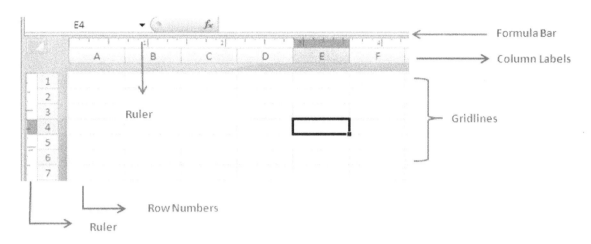

Fig 5.11

Rule: Uncheck this box to hide the ruler. This can only be done when you are on the page layout view. Under the normal view, the ruler will not display.

Message Bar: Uncheck this box to hide the ruler. This can only be done when there are message bar items, otherwise, it will not be available.

Window View

This is slightly different from the Workbook view earlier discussed above. This indicates the appearance of your screen. Under the window view, you will be able to freeze panes, show or hide windows, etc.

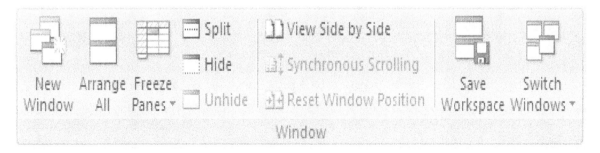

Fig 5.12

- **New Window:** This will simply create a replica of your current view i.e. same screen twice or trice, depending on your choice.

  - **Arrange All:** Arrange all opened workbooks in the required order.

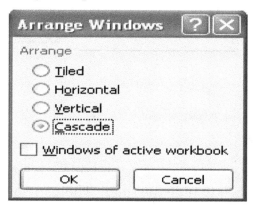

Fig 5.13

The opened workbook can be tiled, arranged horizontally, vertically or even cascaded. Rather than arranging all opened workbook, you can arrange only the worksheet in active workbook by checking the box besides "Windows of active workbook"

- **Freeze Panes:** This is especially useful if you have a large worksheet with so many rows and columns. For instance, if you have data with names on the left column and various headers on the first few rows, you might want to know your current position. In this case, you freeze either the rows or columns or even both. This makes the frozen part permanent while scrolling through other parts of the worksheet.

- **Split:** Divides the window into 4 parts or 2 parts. You can split vertically or horizontally

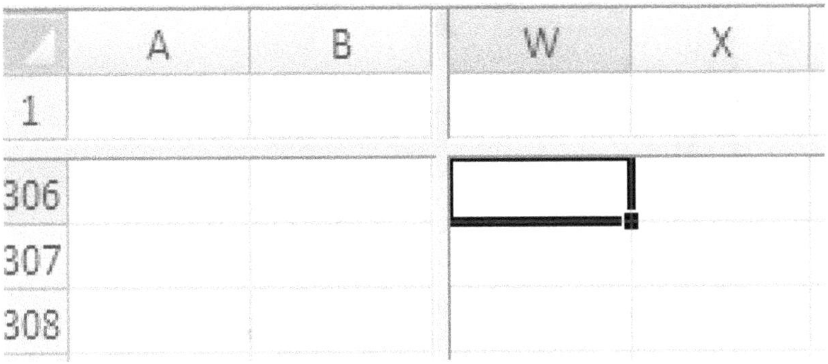

◢	A	B	W	X
1				
306				
307				
308				

Fig 5.14

Above is an excel worksheet split into 4 parts. With this, however wide the spreadsheet is, you can keep columns A & B permanent while working or scrolling through columns C to whatever.

- **Hide:** Click Hide to hide a worksheet window
- **Unhide:** Click unhide to display worksheet window.
- **View Side by Side:** Gives you the opportunity to view two worksheets at the same time. When you click on the icon, it present you with all the opened workbooks where you can select the files you want to view side by side.

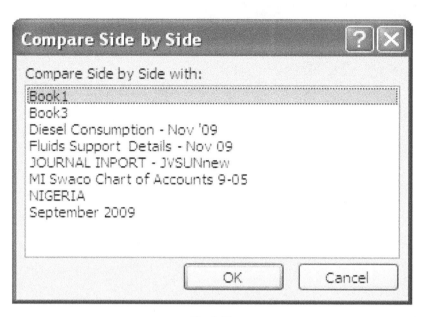

Fig 5.15

- **Synchronous Scrolling:** This will only be enabled if you select view side by side. It simply means that as you move your cursor on one file, the cursor moves on the other file as well. If synchronous scrolling is not clicked, one workbook will be permanent as you scroll through the other.

- **Reset Window Position:** Shares the screen equally between the two files. It is possible that you have given 3 quarters of the screen to one file while the second file has only 1 quarter. If reset window position is clicked, the screen is shared equally.

- **Switch Windows:** Move from one file to the other.

Grouping Worksheets

Grouping worksheets in Excel can be very useful when you plan performing some functions on all worksheets in opened workbook. You can imagine having about 20 worksheets in a workbook and for some reasons, you discovered that you ought to have inserted the company name and address on rows 1 to 4 of each of the worksheets. If you are to do this manually, you have to either correct one of the sheets; then copy the information from one sheet to the other until you get to sheet 20. With worksheet grouping, you can achieve this within one or two minutes. Simply follow the procedure below:

1) Create 3 simple worksheets in the same workbook with the following information:

Sheet1

Sheet 1				Sheet 2				Sheet 3			
Item	qty	SP	Amount	Item	qty	SP	Amount	Item	qty	SP	Amount
sugar	500	30	15000	sugar	700	30	21000	sugar	550	30	16500
milk	400	60	24000	milk	260	60	15600	milk	280	60	16800
salt	560	250	140000	salt	450	250	112500	salt	70	250	17500
Total			179000	Total			149100	Total			50800

Fig 5.16

For the purpose of this exercise, the following assumptions are made:

a) Each of the sheets starts from Item in cell A1 and ends in cell D5.

b) The name of the company and the title of each sheet were erroneously omitted

c) We need to format the columns titled amount and the row titled Total.

2) To accomplish the above task, hold down the shift key and click on sheet 1 and sheet 3. All the three sheets will be selected as a group. Any operation you perform on one will automatically be performed on the others.

3) Highlight rows 1 to 3 and click insert to insert blank rows.

4) Type the name of the company in cell A1 and the title in cell A3

5) Highlight cell D4 to D8 and fill it with yellow color

6) Do the same for cells A8 to D8. Click on bold to format the range.

It is very important to note that once you are in group mode, any operation performed in one sheet will be performed in other

To ungroup the worksheets, just click on any sheet not in the group. Where all the sheets in the file are grouped, click on any worksheet to ungroup,

Creating Multiple Lines in a Cell

It might interest you to know that you can create several lines of texts in a single cell, you can create paragraphs with bullets similar to word documents in Excel. Let's type something that looks like the document below:

"Excel is a very powerful tool that can be used to achieve several objectives with little effort. It is however sad that most people are limiting the package either due to ignorance or training to explore what the application can accomplish. You can achieve the following with little effort:

- Create data that can easily be manipulated without stress. This data can be rearranged, summarized with ease
- You can as well create the chart of the data
- Print the data, etc."

As earlier said, you can type the above in a single cell. To do this, follow the steps below:

1) Format the cell, go to the alignment tab, under text control, click wrap text. This will enable the text to flow.

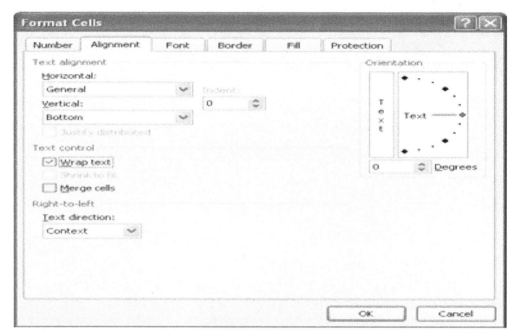

Fig 5.17

2) Enter the text above from "Excel …. Effort:" but do not press Enter key

3) Hold down the Alt + Enter to create a new line

4) To create the bullet, type Alt+0149 and a bullet will appear

   **From the numeric pad please. If you are using a notebook, use Alt+Fn+0149

5) Enter the line "Create data… ease"

6) Repeat steps 3 and 4 until you have enter the enter information.

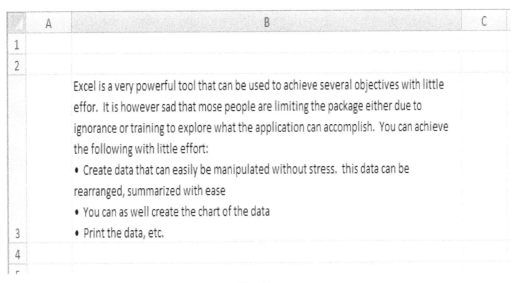

Fig 5.18

Your worksheet should be similar to the above if you follow the instruction.

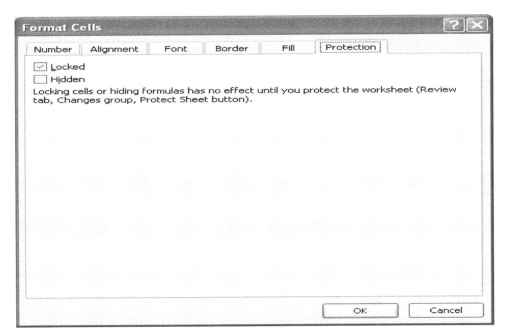

Fig 5.19

Creating Text with Multiple Formats on the same Line

It is possible to create a single line with multiple formats in Microsoft Excel. Let's take a look at the following text:

In the *country* of the blind, an eyed man is the King. To create this in Excel, do the following:

a) Type in the text in Excel

b) Highlight the portion you intend to change and click Font Color and other format required.

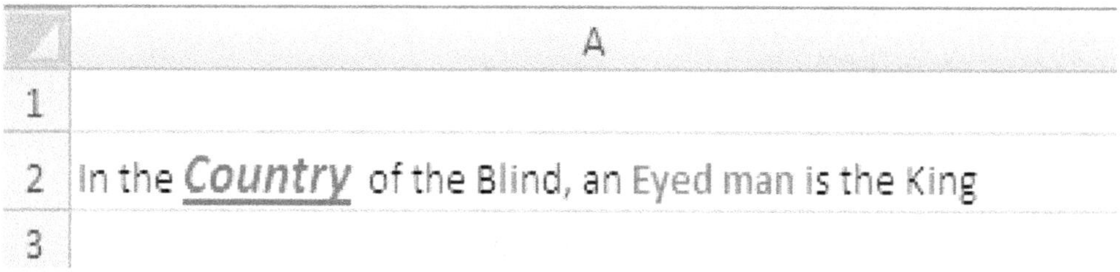

	A
1	
2	In the *Country* of the Blind, an Eyed man is the King
3	

Fig 5.20

6

Copy, Cut & Paste

You will cover:

- *Introduction*
- *Copying or Cutting Cells*
- *Pasting copied information*
- *How to paste special*
- *How to Auto Fill*
- *How to insert Copied cells between columns or rows*

Introduction

In Microsoft Excel, you can copy, cut and paste cell contents, sheets, formulas, charts, etc. Your intention will determine the method you will use. Let's take a look at the first two, copy and cut.

Copy: If your objective is to create a duplicate of a particular range, then you will use copy. This can be achieved by pressing **Ctrl + C**.

Cut: If you are aiming at lifting the information from the current position to another place, cut will be preferable. After highlighting the information, you can press **Ctrl + X** to cut the information or better still use either the mouse or the icon (see diagram below).

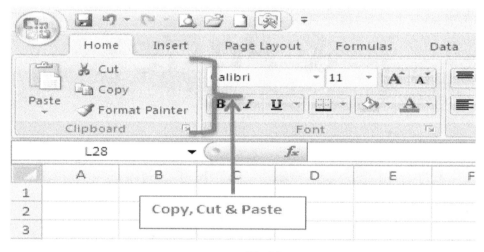

Fig 6.0

Using the button above is simple. Just highlight the information and click Cut, Copy or Format Painter. The information (if copy or cut is clicked) or the format (if Format Painter is clicked) is placed on the clipboard where you can make use of it later.

There are two methods when using the mouse. First is by highlighting the information and clicking the right button of the mouse. This will display the following:

Fig 6.1

Paste:

You can paste the information on the clipboard to any location of your choice in a worksheet. This is the simplest method of pasting such information. You can do this in the following manner:

a) Place the cursor in the cell and press **Ctrl + V**. This is especially helpful when you have several cells that are not together, e.g. You copy an information from cell A1 and you want to place the information on cell A9, B20, B40, C45, etc. If you use **Ctrl + V**, the information is still retained and can be pasted in various cells either pressing **Ctrl + V** in each cell or by holding down your Ctrl and using the mouse pointer to select all the cells and then press **Ctrl + V**.

b) Place the cursor in the cell, right click and select paste from the menu

Paste Special:

Paste Special gives you a variety of options unlike the ordinary Paste discussed above. With Paste Special, you convert to value, formula and even perform mathematical operations. Below is the screen shot of Paste Special:

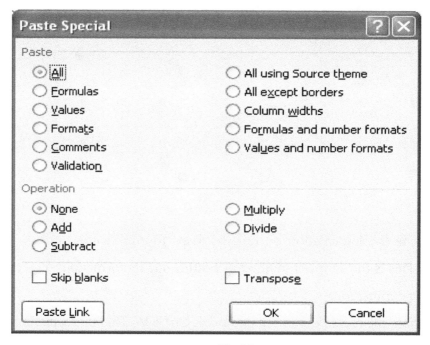

Fig 6.2

The screen is divided into two sections:

Paste

a) All: This gives you the same result as ordinary Paste

b) Formulas: Paste the formula from the copied cell to the current position. Remember that Excel will use relative cell reference when pasting the formula for instance, if the formula in cell C1 = (A1+B1) and you copy cell C1 to cell C3 with paste special (Formulas), your result will be cells (A3+B3).

c) Values: This converts the information you copied to absolute value. Example, if you have 2 in cell a1, 5 in cell A2, 7 in cell A3 and you have a formula =A1+A2+A3 in cell A4 which gives you 14. If you copy cell A4 to cell B4 selecting Values under Paste Special, cell B4 content will be 14 and not the formula.

d) Formats: This pastes only the format from the copied cell to the current cell

e) Comments: This pastes only the comments to the current cell

f) Validation: Pastes only the validation without copying the contents of the cell

g) All using Source theme: Similar to all

h) All except boarders: Similar to all but will not paste the lines

i) Column widths: This increases or decreases the current column to the column width of the copied cell

j) Formulas and number formats: Similar to all but will leave out other formats except number format

k) Values and number formats: Similar to Values but leaves out other formats except number format

Operation

Under Operations, we have:

a) None: No operation is performed at all

b) Add: Adds the copied cell to the contents of the current cell

c) Subtract: Subtracts the copied cell from the contents of the current cell

d) Multiply: Multiplies the contents of the current cell with the copied cell

e) Divide: Divides the current cell by the copied cell

f) Skip Blanks: Omits blank cells and paste only cells that have entries.

g) Transpose: Converts rows to columns or vice versa.

h) Paste Link: Creates a formula with absolute reference to the copied cell.

Insert Copied Cell:

This is another option you can use to paste copied information in the destination cell. For instance, if you copy an entire row, you might want to create a new row with the information on the clipboard, simply highlight and select Insert Copied Cell; a new row will be inserted with your copied information. Entire column behaves the same way. However, if you highlight a single or multiple cells to paste the information and you click on Insert Copied Cell, you will be given the opportunity to decide what you intend to achieve. Simply right click and the screen below will appear:

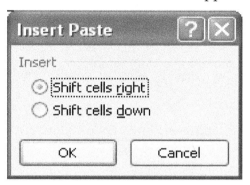

Fig 6.3

Depending on your choice, Excel can shift all other cells down or right to paste your copied information.

Format Painter:

This enables you to copy format from a range or cells to another range. This copies only the format like lines, colors, etc.

Auto Fill:

Auto Fill is another method you can use to copy and paste information in Excel. It is a wonderful tool to use when dealing with information that follows specific pattern for example: 1, 2,3 etc, Jan, Feb, Mar, etc. You can accomplish this by using any of the following methods:

a) Complete the 1st two cells and highlight the cells. Move your cursor to the edge of the cell and your mouse pointer changes to "+". Hold down the left button and continue dragging it till you get to your desired cell. Let's type Jan in cell A1, Feb in cell A2. Format cell A2 to green and leave cell A1 unformatted.

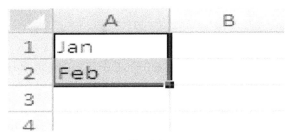

Fig 6.4

b) Place your mouse pointer at the edge of cell A2 until the pointer changes to +. Hold the left button down and drag your mouse until you get to cell A12 and release your mouse. The result should look like this:

Fig 6.5

You will notice that Excel automatically filled cells A3 to A12 with the pattern found in cells A1 and A2.

You might as well want to change the pattern by clicking on auto fill option
. This gives you more options like copy cells, fill series, fill formatting only, fill without formatting, fill months depending on the nature of data. If you use copy cells in the previous example, your output will read Jan, Feb, Jan, Feb instead of Jan to Dec. Fill formatting only will create the format without data:

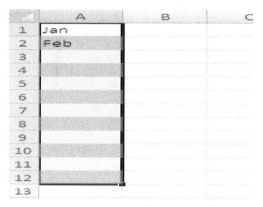

Fig 6.6

Fill without formatting will use your initial information to create your series without copying the format.

If you are dealing with only numbers, fill month will not be displayed.

c) Assessing the Auto Fill under the Editing Menu:

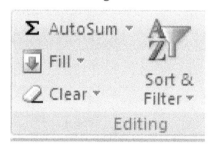

Fig 6.7

Clicking on this gives you options such as Down, Up, Right, Left, Across Worksheets, Series and Justify. We will only consider Across Worksheets and Series:

   a. Across Worksheet will only be enabled if you select more than one worksheet, i.e. you are in a group of worksheet. Once selected, it displays a dialog box where you can select All, Contents or Formats

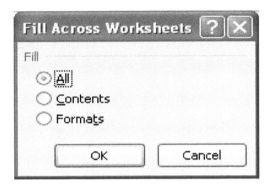

Fig 6.8

All will copy the series in all the selected worksheets.

b. The Series will display a different dialog box below:

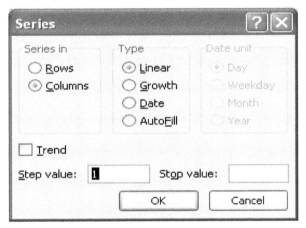

Fig 6.9

You may decide to have your series in rows or column. Under the type, you have linear, growth, date, auto fill. If you select date, the date unit will be enabled. Excel uses the value you entered under the step value to generate the incremental or exponential series.

Notes:

7

Working with Text

You will cover:

- *Introduction*
- *The Left, Middle and Right Functions*
- *The Lower, Upper and Proper Functions*
- *The And/ Or Functions*
- *The Round Functions*
- *The text Functions*

Introduction

If you work with large volume of data, you are likely going to have situations where you intend to extract information from one particular column or merge text from various columns to form a new column. This chapter will expose you to several methods of extracting information. In Excel, we have functions like Left, Right, Middle, Upper, Lower, etc. These are powerful tools or functions that can bail you out when trying to meet deadlines. Each of these functions is explained below:

The LEFT Function

This function extracts information from the left to the right. With this function, you must specify the number of characters or text to extract, otherwise, an error will be triggered. The syntax for left function is:

$$=Left(A1,10)$$

The above will extract information from Cell "A1" starting from the first text or character to the tenth character.

The MID Function

Simply derived from the word middle, it extracts information between the second character and the last character in a cell depending on the length. The syntax is a little different from the left function.

$$=Mid(A1,5,12)$$

The above formula starts extracting information from the 5th character and count 12 characters from that point. Let's assume the information you have in cell A1 is Microsoft Excel, the result of the above formula will be "soft Excel". This can be very useful if you have specific pattern of information and you intend to arrange your data using such information.

The RIGHT Function

This is similar to the left function but extracts information from the right rather than left. The syntax is very similar to the left function

=Right(A1,5)

The above will simply extract 5 rightmost characters from the cell A1.

The LOWER Function

Simply converts the text in the referenced cell to lower case. If you have "Ojo" in Cell A1 and you issue the command, it will be converted to "ojo". The syntax is simply:

=LOWER(A1)

The UPPER Function

This is similar to the lower function but converts to upper case. Syntax is"

=UPPER(A1)

The PROPER Function

This Proper Function converts text using space capital. For example, if you have information like "IN THE COUNTRY OF THE BLIND" in cell A1, you can issue formula like proper to convert it to the correct text without necessarily retyping the information. Simply type the formula:

=PROPER(A1)

The information will be converted to "In The Country Of The Blind"

The TEXT Function:

This converts numbers to texts. This is particularly useful where you intend to combine numbers and texts together to form a word. The format is:

=TEXT(A1,"0.00")

The above formula will convert the numbers in Cell A1 using 2 places of decimal

The VALUE Function:

This converts numbers originally entered or formatted as text to value. This can be a very useful tool when extracting from a cell containing both numbers and texts. When numbers are extracted from text, it is still regarded as text but can be converted to number by the Value function.

=VALUE(A1)

The FIXED Function:

This is an important function for those that may want to program in Excel. It is also useful for the advanced users. The function converts numbers to text. The syntax is simply:

=FIXED(x,y,z)

x represents the Cell or the number

y represents the number of decimals you want

z can be 0 or 1

0 = put comma

1 = don't put comma

Using our example of 19,995.872545.

=FIXED(19,995.872545,2,0) will produce 19,995.87

=FIXED(19,995.872545,2,1) will produce 19995.87

Remember that the result will be text whether you put comma or not.

The INT Function:

This is another important function for programming. This function rounds a number down to the nearest integer. Syntax:

=INT(x) where x represent either the number or cell reference

Example: =INT(19,995.872545) gives 19,995

This can be your saving grace when manipulating data to produce specific result.

The *ROUND* Function

This function rounds numbers to the specified places of decimals. For example, if you have 19,995.872545 and you intend to round it to 2 places of decimals, the round function will cut off the extra decimals and return 19,995.87. The syntax is:

=ROUND(A1,x)

A1 represents the Cell or the number and x represents the places of decimal. In the above example, the formula will be =ROUND(19,995.872545,2)

The *ROUNDUP* function does the same thing with the ROUND function. The *ROUNDDOWN* on the other hand will reduce anything above 0.5 to 0. Using the above example, let's round the figure to 1 place of decimal. This can be achieved using the three options:

=ROUND(19,995.872545,1) will give 19,995.9

=ROUNDUP(19,995.872545,1) will give 19,995.9

=ROUNDDOWN(19,995.872545,1) will give 19,995.8

You have to be careful when using the functions especially the *ROUNDDOWN* function.

The MAX and MIN Function:

If you are a regular user of numbers, you might have fallen into a situation where you have a long list of data and you are looking for the maximum and the minimum for some reasons. The MAX function returns the maximum while the MIN function returns the minimum.

Syntax:=Max(x:y) where x:y represents the range

=MIN(x:y) where x:y represents the range

The & function

This is a very useful character in Excel. You can use it to combine columns, rows, text, etc. When combining text, you cannot use + as this will trigger error but rather use the & sign.

Syntax =(x1 & x2 & x3 .....)

The TRIM function

This function removes all blank spaces before and after the text. For example, " in the country of the blind   " has some spaces before the word in and the word blind. The TRIM function will produce the following:

=TRIM("   in the country of the blind   ") will produce "in the country of the blind"

The LEN function

This function returns the length of text. E.g.

=LEN("Testing") returns 7

The CONCATENATE Function

This function combines texts or cells. It is similar to the & function.

Syntax: =concatenate(x,y,z) where x,y,z are cells or texts.

Go to Excel and type "In the Country of the Blind," in cell A3. Also type "An eyed Man is the King" in cell A4. In Cell A6, type the following formula

=CONCATENATE(A3," ",A4). It will produce the following:

	A	B	C
1			
2			
3	In the Country of the Blind,		
4	An eyed Man is the King		
5			
6	In the Country of the Blind, An eyed Man is the King		
7			

Fig 7.0

The COUNT Function

This counts the number of cells in a range that contains numbers.

Syntax : =COUNT(RANGE)

Example: Enter 45, 42 and 50 in cells B2, B3 and B4 respectively. Enter '70, John and James in cells B5, B6 and B7 respectively. Make cells B5 to B7 right aligned and type the formula in cell B9

=COUNT(B2:B7) and you will get 3

You are getting 3 because of the following:

- COUNT function counts only cells with numbers
- Even though you typed 70 in cell B5 but Excel will not see it as number because of the ['] in from of the 70. As a result, it is seen as text despite the fact that you made it right aligned.

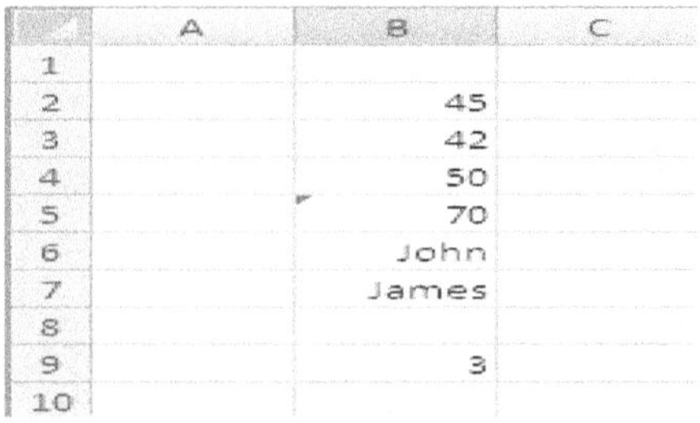

	A	B	C
1			
2		45	
3		42	
4		50	
5		70	
6		John	
7		James	
8			
9		3	
10			

Fig 7.1

The COUNTA Function

It counts the number of non blank cells and returns the value

The beauty of Excel is that you can combine some of these functions together to facilitate your data entry or manipulation.

THE LOGICAL FUNCTIONS

The AND Function

This is a good function that you can use to manipulate data. It confirms whether all arguments are true.

Syntax: =AND(arg1,arg2,arg3,etc) where arg1,arg2,etc are logical statements or cells

It returns **TRUE** or **FALSE**. True if all the conditions are met but false even if one of the argument does not meet any of the conditions. In the example below, use a blank sheet, highlight cells A3 to C4. Type 45 and press Ctrl + Enter to fill the entire selection with 45. Change cell A4 to 42 and type the =AND(A3=45,B3=45,C3=45). Copy the formula to cell D4 and your result should look like the one below:

	A	B	C	D	E
1					
2					
3	45	45	45	TRUE	
4	42	45	45	FALSE	
5					
6					
7					

Fig 7.2

Cell D4 is false because cell A4 equals 42 and not 45.

The OR Function

This is similar to the AND function but the difference is that it returns True if any of the arguments meets the condition.

Syntax:

=OR(arg1,arg2,arg3,etc) where arg1,arg2,etc are logical statements or cells

It returns **TRUE** or **FALSE**. True if any of the conditions are met but false if none of the conditions are met. Use the same example above but change the formula in cell D3 to

=OR(A3=45,B3=45,C3=45). Copy the formula to cell D4 and your result should look like the one below:

	A	B	C	D
1				
2				
3	45	45	45	TRUE
4	42	45	45	TRUE
5				

Fig 7.3

Both Cells D3 and D4 will be True even though A4 is 42 but since B4 is 45, the output will be True.

The ABS Function

This function returns the absolute value ignoring the signs e.g. ABS(50.50) returns 50.50 and ABS(-50.50) returns 50.50 as well.

The ISBLANK Function

This function simply checks if a cell is blank and it returns True or False.

Syntax: =ISBLANK(value) . The value could be cell reference

Using the above example:

=ISBLANK(A2) will produce TRUE while

=ISBLANK(A3) will produce FALSE

ISERR /ISERROR

At times, when you entered formula in Excel, you get error message not necessarily because your formula Is wrong but could be due to the data you are using. For example, you are dividing column A with the information in column B. If any of the values in column is 0, you will get an error message like "#DIV/0!" and at times you get "#VALUE!" depending on the mathematical function you are using. ISERR OR ISERROR function can be used to determine which cell contains error message. With the result, you can filter only the error cells for investigation or correction or better still, you might even filter only the non-error cells for your purpose.

Syntax: ISERR(xx) where xx represents the cell or value

        ISERROR(xx) where xx represents the cell or value

You will appreciate the importance of these functions if you are working with data of about 5000 to 10000 rows and you have to use either the arrow keys or page up and down to determine which cell contains error message unlike when you are working with 500 lines.

Example:

Enter the following information in Excel:

Class	Total Age of Pupils in class	No of Pupils in the class	Average age in the class
1a	180	20	
1b	135	15	
2a	190		
2b	185	20	
3a	150		
3b	170	20	

Press space bar in cell C4 on the assumption that you erroneously press space instead of entering number and leave cell C6 blank. Let's use formula to determine the average age. Arrange the above in Excel and enter the following formula in cell D2:

=B2/C2

Copy the formula down to D7. Type "Total in cell A8 and click ∑ in cell B8 to automatically type =SUM(B2:B7) and copy the formula down to D8. Your worksheet should look like this:

	A	B	C	D
1	Class ▾	Total Age of Pupils in cla ▾	No of Pupils in the cla ▾	Average age in the cla ▾
2	1a	180	20	9
3	1b	135	15	9
4	2a	190		#VALUE!
5	2b	185	20	9.25
6	3a	150		#DIV/0!
7	3b	170	20	8.5
8	Total	1010	75	#VALUE!

Fig 7.4

You will observe that column D has some errors and as a result, cell D8 has error too. If you have various types of errors in column D and the data spans to thousands of rows, it will be difficult to know the rows containing errors. Enter the following in cell E2 and copy it down to cell E7.

=ISERROR(D2) or =ISERR(D2)

	A	B	C	D	E
1	Class ▾	Total Age of Pupils in cla ▾	No of Pupils in the cla ▾	Average age in the cla ▾	▾
2	1a	180	20	9	FALSE
3	1b	135	15	9	FALSE
4	2a	190		#VALUE!	TRUE
5	2b	185	20	9.25	FALSE
6	3a	150		#DIV/0!	TRUE
7	3b	170	20	8.5	FALSE
8	Total	1010	75	#VALUE!	
9					

Fig 7.5

With that, you can filter using column E to display all rows with error messages in column D.

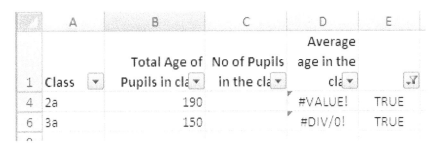

	A	B	C	D	E
1	Class	Total Age of Pupils in cla	No of Pupils in the cla	Average age in the cla	
4	2a	190		#VALUE!	TRUE
6	3a	150		#DIV/0!	TRUE

Fig 7.6

You can then enter the correct information in the various cells. Some will filter on column D instead of E but the fact remains that you will have to do that for each type of errors but is far easier and faster to use the first method.

The IF Function

This function checks if a condition is met and returns True, if the condition is not met, it returns False. One nice thing about this function is the fact that you can combine this function with other functions and can even be nested.

Syntax: =IF(Logical_Test, what to do if condition is true, what to do if condition is false)

Example: The information below shows the name and age of some people. In column C, we will use the IF function to determine whether an individual is an adult or infant. Anyone who is 18 and above will be adult while those below 18 are regarded as infant.

	A	B	C
1	Name	A	
2	John	20	
3	James	14	
4	Ope	18	
5	Moses	23	
6	Charles	12	
7	David	22	
8	Total	109	
9			

Fig 7.7

Enter the formula below in cell C2 and copy it down through cell C7

=IF(B2>=18,"Adult",Infant)

Your output will look like this:

	A	B	C
1	Name ▼	A ▼	Class
2	John	20	Adult
3	James	14	Infant
4	Ope	18	Adult
5	Moses	23	Adult
6	Charles	12	Infant
7	David	22	Adult
8	Total	109	
9			

Fig 7.8

8
Range Names

You will cover:

- *Introduction*
- *Name Box*
- *Define Range Name*
- *Name Manager*
- *Creating from Selection*

Introduction

At the beginning of this book, we defined a range as a cell or combination of cells i.e. a range could be just cell A1 or cell A1 to M50. When you have array of data covering several rows and columns or you even have several sheets in a workbook or a particular portion of a worksheet will be referenced always, It might become necessary to name that portion for ease of reference.

Using a layman example, range names could be regarded as groups of students either in a class or school. Each student has his or her unique name and group could be named Chess Club, Red Cross, etc. Each time you mention the name, the students know who you are talking about.

Range names are very useful when performing a search, when working with VLOOKUP or HLOOKUP and can easily be assessed.

Creating Range Names

You can create range names in four different ways:

a) Using the Name Box

b) Using the Define Name Icon

c) Using the Name Manager

d) Create from Selection

Using the Name Box

To create a range name using the Name Box, simply do the following:

- Highlight the range you intend to name
- Click inside the Name Box (see below)
- Type the desired Name

- Press Enter to complete the process. Note that without pressing the Enter key, the name you typed in will be discarded.

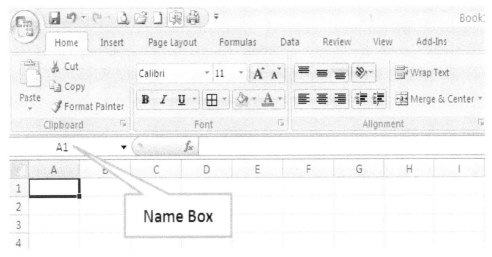

Fig 8.0

Using Define Name

To create a range name using this method, do the following:

- Select Formulas from the Main Menu and click on Define name. The New Name dialog box appears:

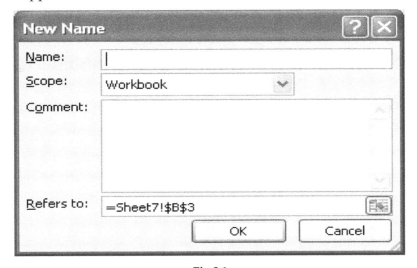

Fig 8.1

- **Name:** type the name you intend to give the range

- **Scope:** whether local or global. Local can be reference from the same worksheet but must be qualified before you can reference it from other worksheet in the same workbook. Global name can be referenced from any part of the workbook

- **Comment:** if you have any comment

- **Refers to:** the cell reference e.g. B2:L13

- Click OK to accept your entries

Once you have defined the range name, you can now use the name manager to modify or edit the parameters of the name. To test the range name you have created, go to any part of the worksheet and click the name from the name box, Excel automatically takes you to the beginning of the range. You will know the importance of this when we treat lookup and other mathematical functions.

Name Manager

You can also create a range name using the Name Manager. In addition, it enables you to delete or edit names already created using any of the methods. To create, edit or delete names using Name Manager, do the following:

a) Select Formulas from the Main Menu and click on Name Manager. The Name Manager dialog box appears:

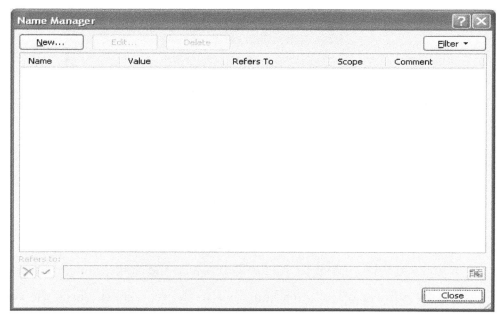

Fig 8.2

b) From the above dialog box, the Edit and Delete buttons are disabled because no Range Name has been created.

c) Click New to create a new name and a New Name dialog box earlier discussed above appears. Complete the dialog box and click OK.

You can edit or delete range names with the Name Manager.

Creating Range Name from Selection

You can also create a range name using "Create from Selection" under the Define Name icons. The system simply uses row headings, column labels to generate your range names. To do this, follow the steps below:

• Select Formulas from the Main Menu and click on Create from Selection and "Create Names from Selection" dialog box appear.

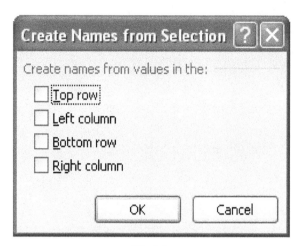

Fig 8.3

- If you want the system to use the Top row as the range names and create names for the number of columns and rows in the worksheet, check the box besides **"Top Row"**

9

Formatting Cells

You will cover:

- *Introduction*
- *Using Fonts*
- *Lines and Borders*
- *Colors*
- *Alignments*
- *Orientation*
- *Indentation*

Introduction

Presentation is an important aspect of any job. No matter how detailed or complex your worksheet is, people may not appreciate the efforts and time spent doing the job if not properly presented. It is therefore important to format and present your work in a professional manner. Formatting your work involves the following:

1) Using the appropriate Font
2) Lines and Grids
3) Use of Color
4) Alignment
5) Protection
6) Number, etc.

Using Appropriate Fonts

There are so many Fonts you can choose from in Microsoft Excel. You can access Fonts through the icons on the Ribbon or by clicking the right button of your mouse.

Accessing by the icons on the Ribbon

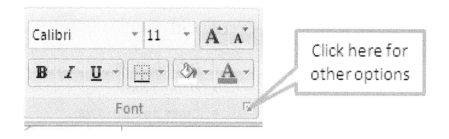

Fig 9.0

From the above diagram, "Calibri" is the current font and 11 is the size. If you click on the arrow besides Calibri, you will have a drop down list of fonts while the arrow besides 11 gives you various sizes. Alternatively, you can click on the A A to either increase or decrease the size of your fonts. B makes the selected text bold while *I* turns the selected text italics. U underlines the selected text and the arrow besides it gives you the option of single underline or double underline. rules the selected cell at the bottom while the arrow besides it gives you more options for borders. paints the selected cell while the arrow besides it gives you more color for the cell. A changes the color of the selected text while the arrow besides it gives you more color options. The arrow beside the word Font presents you with the same formatting options with the right button of your mouse.

Accessing by the right Button of the Mouse

To access the Fonts using this method, click the right button of your mouse and select Format Cells. Click on the Font Tab and the following will appear:

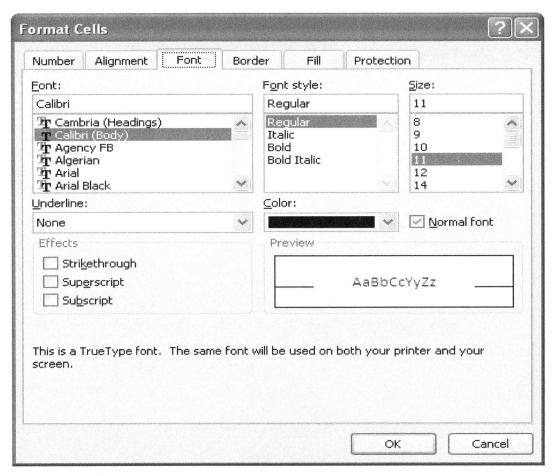

Fig 9.1

Under the Font, you have various fonts to select from. You can use Regular, Italic, Bold or Bold Italic under the style. There are four options under underline: Single, Double, Single Accounting and Double Accounting. The difference between Single and Single Accounting is that Single will underline the text while Single Accounting will underline the entire cell. Double underlines the text and Double Accounting underlines the entire cell. It is also important to point out that Single Accounting and Double Accounting are also different from the regular line method in the sense that when you use line instead of font, the line remains even if the text is deleted but if you use single or double accounting, the entire line disappears once the text is deleted.

Effect can be Strikethrough **A** or Superscript ᴬ or Subscript ₐ. You can choose any color from the color chart. The Preview displays how your output will appear when printed. It is important to note that your printer has a lot to do with font availability.

Lines and Borders

In Microsoft Excel, you can apply borders to the currently selected cells or range by clicking on the icon located in the Ribbon. The icon displays the last border used and can be bottom, top, left, right, all, etc. The arrow beside the borders displays the following where you can make other choices:

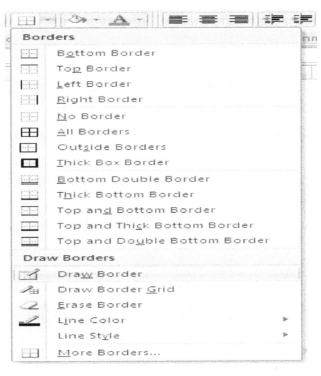

Fig 9.2

You can also access the Borders by clicking your right mouse, click Format Cells and go to the Border Tab. This gives you more options than the one earlier discussed.

Colors:

You can fill a cell or range with any color or colors of your choice. You can also change the color of your fonts, the lines and borders, etc.

Alignment:

Alignment enables you to arrange your text in various ways. You can align your text vertically or horizontally. Below are the alignment icons from the Ribbon.

Fig 9.3

Below are the results of clicking on the icons:

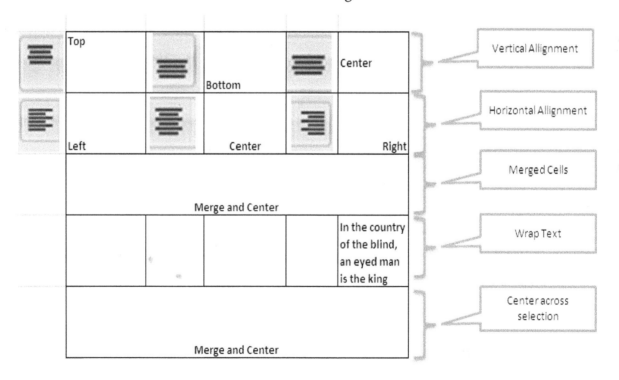

Fig 9.4

Note the following when aligning information:

1) Text will flow across to the previous or next cell if the text is longer than the cell. Numbers will not overflow.

2) When you merge cells, there are operations you can no longer perform e.g. cut a cell.

Orientation:

This enables you to rotate text in a diagonal or vertical form. Click on and the following screen appears:

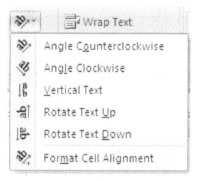

Fig 9.5

Preview of each of the options is on the left hand side of the above diagram.

Indentation:

Each cell in a worksheet can be formatted to create increase or decrease indentation. shifts your text forward slightly while shifts the indent backward a little

The Number Format

This is applicable to numbers. Numbers can be formatted to decimal places, percentage, currency, or even as text.

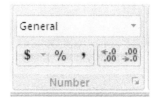

Fig 9.6

From the above, General indicates that there is no specific format. The arrow besides General gives you various options such as accounting, date, decimal, etc. The **$** represents currency while the arrow besides it gives you more currencies. % represents percentage. **,** automatically applies comma on thousands. increases decimal while decreases decimal.

If you click the right button of your mouse and select Format Cell, then go to the number tab, you have more options. You can also access this by clicking on the arrow besides Number.

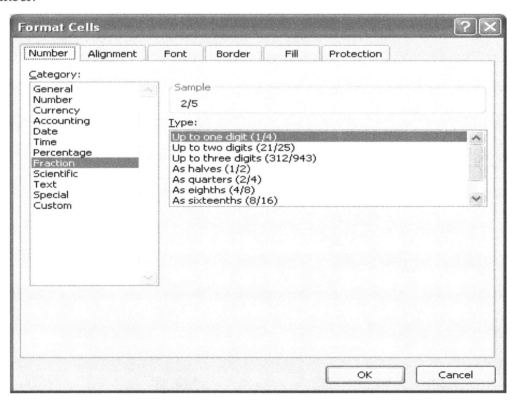

Fig 9.7

You can use scientific, text, special format or create a custom format.

You will also be able to see the preview of the applicable format.

Protection:

Protection under format cell will only be effective if your worksheet is protected and there are basically two options:

Locked: If this is enabled, user of your worksheet will not be able to type information on the cells if the worksheet is protected. If it is not enabled, the cells with the format will allow data input.

Hidden: If enabled, the cells will be hidden once the worksheet is protected.

Notes:

10

Protection and Sharing

You will cover:

- *Introduction*
- *Protecting your File*
- *Protecting your Workbook/Worksheet*
- *Sharing Workbook*
- *Tracking Changes*

Introduction

Protection in Microsoft Excel comes in two ways. Either you want to protect the entire file in which case, unauthorized user will not have access at all or you want to protect workbook or worksheet. When you protect a workbook or a worksheet, the users have access to the information but may not be able to modify such workbook. We will discuss both protections in detail

Protecting your File

In recent times, protecting your information can be very valuable especially where you use shared resources like network, office computers, etc. If files are not protected, people can gain unauthorized access to your confidential files and share the information with your competitors, friends, union members, etc. We have seen where people hacked into personal computers of others and stole their business ideas, confidential information about them and cause major setback for such individuals.

Apart from the normal protection from windows through log on IDs and Passwords, Screen Savers, Microsoft Excel has its own in-built protection that can be used to protect your file. Once implemented, you will be required to supply your password to open the file or modify the file.

To protect your file, do the following:

1) Click on the Office Button and click Save As. Select the format you want from the list of formats. The following dialog box appears:

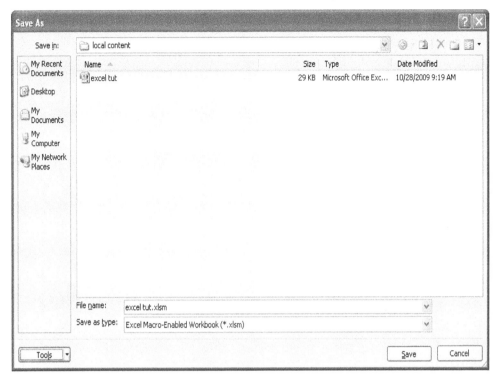

Fig 10.0

2) Check Save in and ensure you have the correct directory and folder.

3) Change the file name if different from the suggested name

4) Select your desired file type

5) Click on Tools and select General Options. The general option dialog box appears.

Fig 10.1

6) Type the Password to open

7) Type the Password to modify.

8) If you want the file to be Read Only, tick or check the "Read-only recommended" box. If you want to create a backup, check the "Always create backup" box.

9) Click OK to close the General Options

10) You will be requested to confirm the password

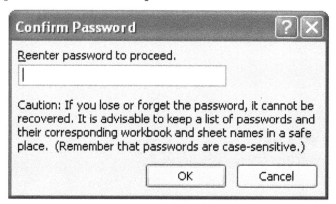

Fig 10.2

Retype the password and click OK to

11) Click Save to complete the process.

Once you have completed the process, close the file and open it again. The following dialog box appears;

Fig 10.3

You must enter the correct password to be able to open or modify the file. If you enter the wrong password, you will receive the following error message:

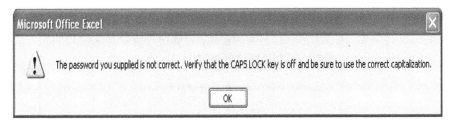

Fig 10.4

Protecting Workbook or Worksheet

Contrary to the kind of protection earlier discussed where unauthorized user will be completely denied access to your file, workbook or worksheet protection is slightly different. In this case, the user has access to the file but may not be able to modify all or part of the file. This is of great importance when you are designing input form with some preset information that you will not want the user to modify or amend. You can also use this method where you have some worksheet for consolidation and users have to complete the information for their unit with a standard format.

To protect your worksheet, do the following:

1) Make sure you unlock all the cells you want the users to be able to amend (see page 123)

2) Select Review from the main menu and click on Protect Worksheet from the Ribbon and the following screen will appear:

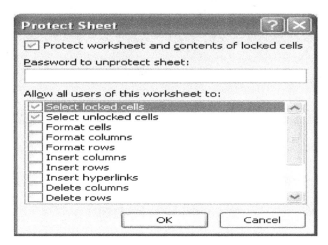

Fig 10.5

If you tick Select Locked Cells above, the user will be able to move the cursor on any cell but will not be able to do anything on the cell. If you however uncheck Select locked Cells, the users will not be able to place cursor on cells and they cannot modify. Just tick anything you want the users to do.

3) Enter Password to unprotect sheet and click OK

4) Confirm your password and click OK

Exercise:

Open a new worksheet and do the following:

a) Type "Enter your Code in cell A1: "

   Type "Enter your Name: " in cell A2:

b) Format cells B1 to B2 as follows:

   Highlight cells B1 to B2 by pressing the right button of your mouse to display Custom Lists. Go to the tab "Fill" and select yellow as the color

   Go to the tab "Protection" and uncheck "Locked". Click OK to close the Custom Lists.

c) Select Review from the main menu and click on Protect Worksheet

d) Uncheck Select Locked Cells and provide your password

e) Click OK to close the dialog box.

Make an attempt to type information on any part of the worksheet except the area earlier formatted as yellow, you will receive the following error message:

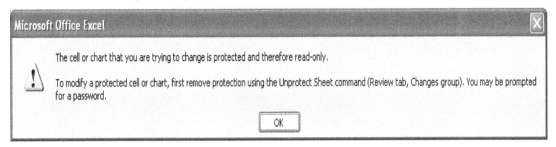

Fig 10.6

Type information where you highlighted yellow and you will not receive any error message.

Sharing Your Workbook

Sharing in Microsoft Excel enables people to have concurrent access to an Excel Workbook at the same time. All of you can make changes to the file provided you are not on the same cell in which case a conflict will occur. This is highly useful where you have various departments updating master file with departmental information e.g. budget file.

To share your workbook, simply follow the steps below:

Click Review and select Share Workbook

Fig 10.7

a) Go to Editing Tab and check Allow changes by more than one user at the same time.

b) Click Advanced Tab to set other parameters such as how to track changes, how to update changes, how to handle conflicting changes between users and others.

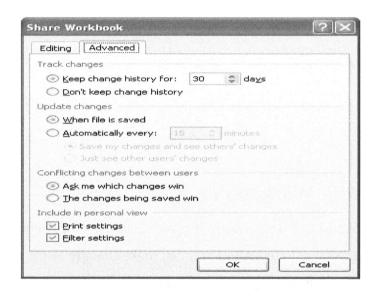

Fig 10.8

c) Click OK to complete the process.

Track Changes

This is another valuable tool in Microsoft Excel. It is used to keep track of modifications to worksheets most especially where such worksheets move from one person to the other for updates or modifications. Changes will be highlighted for you to accept or reject. When you accept, it becomes permanent but will be discarded if rejected.

To track changes, select Review from the main menu and click Track Changes and the following dialog box will appear:

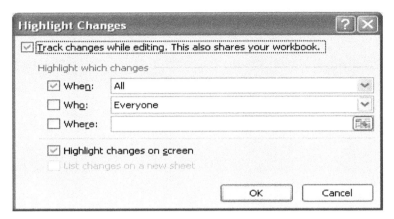

Fig 10.9

Complete your settings and click OK to accept.

Notes:

11
Sorting Your Data

You will cover:

- *Introduction*
- *Auto Sorting without options*
- *The Sort Dialog Box*
- *Practical Demonstration*

Introduction

This is the process of organizing or arranging data for specific purposes. Sorting in Excel can be combined with other functions to achieve high level of efficiency. It might interest you to know that you can sort by the following:

- Entire column or combination of columns
- Partial text in column
- Color of the font
- Color of the cell
- Cell icon.

Before sorting any data, let's review how to sort data first. The icon for sorting data is located under the Data menu. There you will see the following three icons:

This will sort your selection automatically in the ascending order without settings, i.e. starting from the lowest to the highest

This will sort your selection automatically in the descending order without settings, i.e. starting from the highest to the lowest.

This enables you to sort based on your desired options. When you click this icon, the Sort Dialog Box appears:

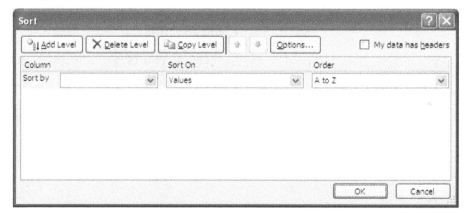

Fig 11.0

Let's review the items on the Sort Dialog Box above;

Add Level:

Generally, you are presented with just one level when you click the Sort Icon. However, it is possible you want to sort a data using different sort criteria; in that case it will be highly useful to create additional sort criteria by adding a new level. For example, you may decide to sort the data on page 154 by Town and by product. The above dialog box only has one level which in this case will be the town. To achieve your goal, you need to add another level by simply clicking add level and picking product as the second sort criteria.

Delete Level :

Clicking this button will delete additional sort criteria you no longer require

Copy Level :

Simply copies the upper level to a new level

The UP and Down Arrows:

The arrows will enable you to move levels up or down i.e. change the position of the sort criteria. This will be very useful where you have several levels and you have decided to change the order of sorting.

Options:

Display the following

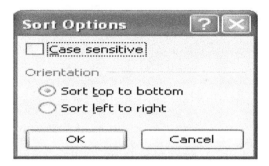

Fig 11.1

You may decide to sort from top to bottom or from left to right and it may even be case sensitive. However, if you tick case sensitive, "A" and "a" are two different letters and will be arranged differently.

My data has headers:

Do not check this if your data is not properly labeled. In that case, Excel will display the column label under the "Sort on", otherwise, the first row of your data will be used as header and the row will be excluded from your data.

Sort by:

Your primary column or any other column you are picking as your sort criteria

Sort on:

This could be by Value (contents of the column), cell color, Font color or Cell icon Order: this could be:

- A to Z i.e. ascending
- Z to A i.e. Descending
- Custom List: where you create your own list. The custom list looks like this:

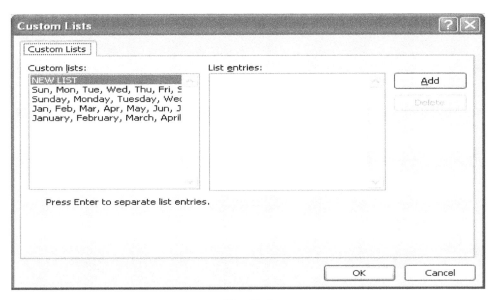

Fig 11.2

We can now demonstrate sorting using our data in page 154 by doing the following:

a) Highlight the entire rows 1 to 49

b) Select Data from the Main menu and click on Sort. The Sort dialog box appears

c) Check the box besides "My data has header". If this box is not checked, Excel displays the column labels to sort data.

d) Under Sort By, select Town, Select Value under Sort On and select A to Z under Order

e) Click Add Label to create additional criteria. Under Sort by, select Product, select value under Sort On and select A to Z under Order

f) Click OK to complete the process

Compare the output with your original data.

Notes:

12

Data Validation

You will cover:

- *Introduction*
- *Setting Up Data Validation*
- *Input Message*
- *Creating Error Messages and Alert*

Introduction

For some of you that are familiar with programming, it is possible to create a master file with references to other files to reduce time spent by your computer in retrieving information. For example, let's assume you are creating a payroll file for your organization. Your master file could look like this:

	A	B	C	D	E	F	G	H	I	J	K
1	Surname	First Name	Middle Name	State of Origin	Local Govt	Date of Birth	Tel No	Dept	Basic	Housing	
2											
3											
4											
5											
6											
7											
8											
9											

Fig 12.0

In the example above, rather than typing Ekiti, Jigawa, Akwa Ibom, etc, you may decide to create range with all the States of the Federation, another range for all the departments in the company, etc. Each record will now have a unique code with detailed description and reference will now be made to the range containing the information on the worksheet. With this method, your data entry becomes reduced, the size of your file becomes smaller and the speed of retrieving information becomes faster. Let's create two more tables (state and department) to demonstrate this:

	A	B	C
1	Department Table		
2			
3	dp_code	dp_name	dp_head
4	DP001	Accounts	Dave James
5	DP002	Admini	Jack Robinson
6	DP003	Engineering	George Rock
7			

	A	B	C
1	State Table		
2			
3	st_code	st_name	st_population
4	001	Lagos	15 Million
5	002	Ogun	5 Million
6	003	Oyo	10 Million
7			

Fig 12.1

In the master file above, it will no longer be necessary to enter the name of the state or department whenever you are in those columns. All you simply need to do is to type in the code corresponding to the state or department and the system can pick the correct names for the state and the department.

However, it is important to note that data input could nullify the benefit of any good design if each field is not restricted to the appropriate types of data. We have seen instances where numbers were entered instead of characters, where digits were omitted from telephone numbers and non existing department or account codes entered, etc. Data validation helps users of such worksheet to know the appropriate data to use as well as the format.

In Excel, Data Validation is located under the Data Tools:

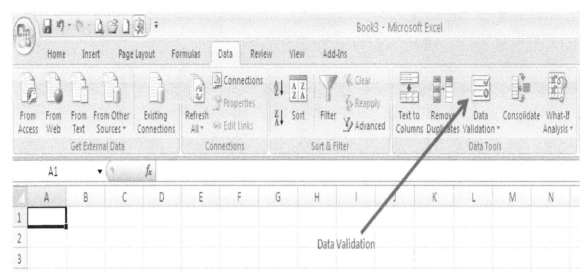

Fig 12.2

On clicked, a dialog box will appear that will guide you:

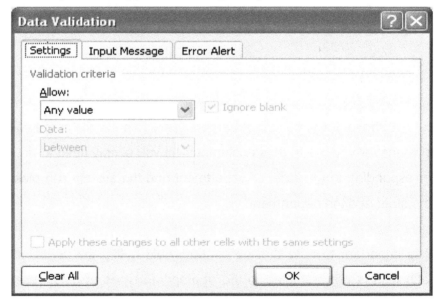

Fig 12.3

There are three tabs: Settings, Input Message and Error alert:

Settings

Under the settings is where you have the validation criteria. Clicking on the Combo Box under "Allow" will display the list of parameters you can set to restrict data input by any user. The following dialog box will be displayed:

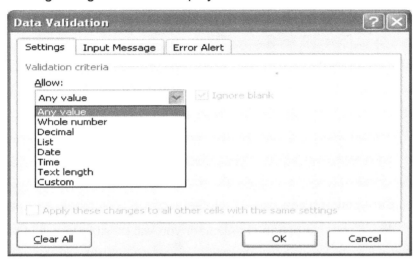

Fig 12.4

Each of them will be explained below:

- **Any Value**

  This is as good as not implementing data restriction. It will simply allow any value including number or character.

- **Whole number**

  This will only allow whole number without decimal point or negative sign. Once selected, it gives you more options to restrict user inputs:

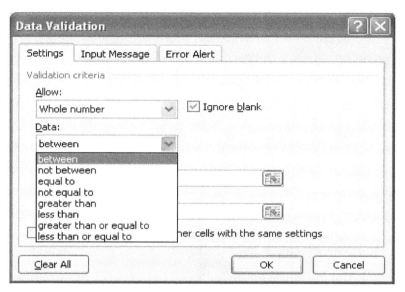

Fig 12.5

- **Between:** You can use this to set a range of numbers for example 25 and 45. Once this option is selected, you will be able to select your minimum and maximum integer and any input outside this range will be rejected. Depending on your set parameters, an error message could be triggered. However, if you enter any number between 25 and 45, the input will be accepted and no error message will be displayed.

- **Not Between:** The opposite of between. In this case, any whole number below 25 and above 45 will be accepted as correct input and 25 to 45 will be rejected.

- **Equal To:** This will display only one field for you to enter the exact figure.

- **Not Equal To:** Any whole number that is not equal to the value entered.

- **Greater Than:** Only whole number greater than the value set will be accepted.

- **Less than:** Only whole number lower than the number set will be accepted.

- **Greater Than or Equal To:** Accepts values higher or equal to the number set.

- **Less Than or Equal To:** Accepts figures less or equal to the figures set.

These options are all applicable to the validation criteria.

- **Decimal**

  The major difference between whole number and Decimal is the fact that any other number other than decimal will be rejected.

- **List**

  With this option, it is possible to create a list of available entries for user to pick or type in the list box. Once selected, a dialog box with Source will appear for you to either enter the values manually or make reference to selected range of cells. Any value outside the list will be rejected. To create a list in the Data Validation screen, select List and type your options separated with comma.

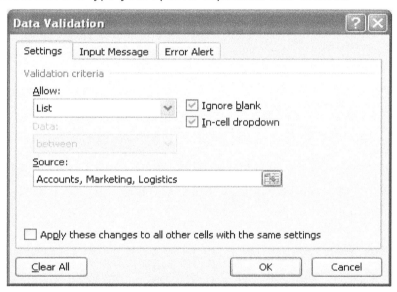

Fig 12.6

Another method you can use is to create the list of acceptable option in a range and make reference to the range:

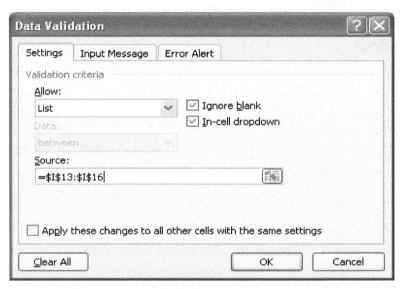

Fig 12.7

- **Date**: Will accept only date
- **Time**: Will accept only time
- **Text Length**: Will accept number or length of the text
- **Custom**: Define your own criteria

You can also apply the changes to all other cells with the same settings by checking the box beside it. You can also instruct the system to ignore blank.

Input Message

The input message box enables you to type a message to display on the screen whenever a user selects the cell with data validation. You can type a title for the message displayed under title and the real message under input message. Once the cell is selected, the message is displayed. Below is the Input Message dialog box.

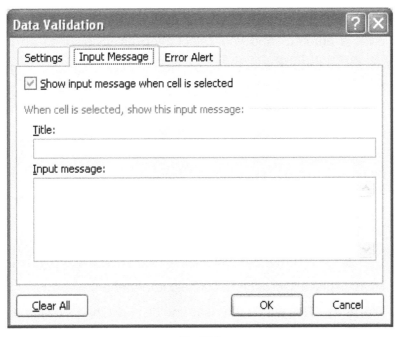

Fig 12.8

Error Alert

This enables Excel to show error alert when an invalid data is entered. The dialog box below shows the Error Alert. It is divided into three major part:

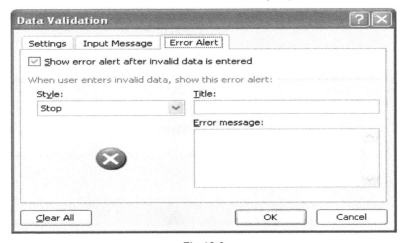

Fig 12.9

- **Style**: There are three options under style vis Stop, Warning and Information.

a. Stop: See the screen above. If you check "Show error alert after invalid data is entered" and you select Stop as style, once an invalid entry is made, an error message will be displayed with the following options:

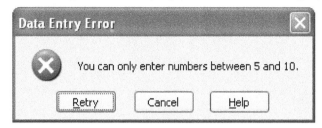

Fig 12.10

Retry will return you to the cell to enter new data

Cancel will return the original information and discard your input

Help displays Microsoft Excel help information.

b. **Warning:** This warns the user and displays the following error message:

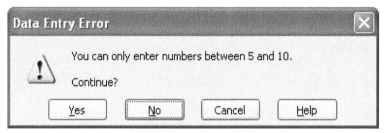

Fig 12.11

If you click yes, the system ignores the error and continues. If you click No, the system returns you back to the cell to make necessary changes. If you click Cancel, the original input will be restored and your input rejected. Help displays help information.

c. **Information:** This will only display information about the error with the following dialog box:

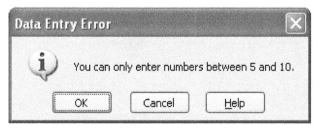

Fig 12.12

Click Ok to accept the invalid data, Cancel to reject your input and return the original entry in the cell. Help to display help information.

Notes:

13

Data Sub-Total

Creating Subtotal

If you have a very long list of information with numeric data say for instance a departmental store that sells various items at various locations, one of the challenges faced by the accounting group is the ability to summarize the various revenue generated by each location either by products, by region, sales group, etc. This can easily be achieved using the subtotal function in Excel. How does it work in Excel? Following are the steps required:

1. Arrange or sort your data

2. Ensure the columns are properly labeled. Although, you can still group your data without label but you get the best result by labeling the column

3. Highlight the rows

4. Click subtotal and a dialog box will appear that will guide you through the process.

Let practice the above with the information extracted from a company that has 4 locations, Lagos, Epe, Badagry and Victoria Island. The company sells 3 products with 4 salesmen. Following are the data extracted from the company's sales record:

Town	Salesman	Product	Qty	Unit Cost	Total
Epe	James	Milk	5000	45	225000
Lagos Island	Andrew	Butter	8500	250	2125000
Victoria Island	Andrew	Milk	9860	45	443700
Victoria Island	Stephen	Sugar	7450	120	894000
Victoria Island	James	Milk	12000	45	540000
Victoria Island	James	Sugar	5600	120	672000
Epe	Stephen	Sugar	2500	120	300000
Epe	James	Butter	4500	250	1125000
Badagry	Stephen	Sugar	3600	120	432000
Badagry	James	Butter	5900	250	1475000
Lagos Island	James	Butter	8000	250	2000000
Epe	Andrew	Butter	5800	250	1450000
Lagos Island	Andrew	Milk	7000	45	315000

Lagos Island	Andrew	Sugar	56000	120	6720000
Badagry	James	Milk	1400	45	63000
Badagry	Andrew	Butter	14950	250	3737500
Victoria Island	James	Butter	4500	250	1125000
Victoria Island	Andrew	Sugar	4870	120	584400
Epe	Stephen	Butter	9000	250	2250000
Lagos Island	Thomas	Milk	9800	45	441000
Victoria Island	Andrew	Butter	3500	250	875000
Badagry	Stephen	Butter	4500	250	1125000
Lagos Island	Thomas	Sugar	3500	120	420000
Lagos Island	James	Milk	6000	45	270000
Epe	Thomas	Milk	800	45	36000
Victoria Island	Thomas	Milk	4800	45	216000
Badagry	Thomas	Milk	3600	45	162000
Lagos Island	Thomas	Butter	9500	250	2375000
Victoria Island	Thomas	Sugar	6500	120	780000
Epe	Stephen	Milk	7500	45	337500
Lagos Island	Stephen	Milk	14000	45	630000
Badagry	Stephen	Milk	7800	45	351000
Lagos Island	Stephen	Sugar	9500	120	1140000
Victoria Island	Thomas	Butter	1200	250	300000
Lagos Island	Stephen	Butter	8500	250	2125000
Victoria Island	Stephen	Milk	9800	45	441000
Lagos Island	James	Sugar	15000	120	1800000
Victoria Island	Stephen	Butter	2360	250	590000
Epe	Andrew	Sugar	4590	120	550800
Badagry	Andrew	Sugar	2500	120	300000
Epe	Thomas	Sugar	7000	120	840000
Badagry	Thomas	Sugar	7400	120	888000
Epe	Andrew	Milk	7000	45	315000
Badagry	Andrew	Milk	7866	45	353970
Epe	Thomas	Butter	3500	250	875000
Epe	James	Sugar	9000	120	1080000
Badagry	Thomas	Butter	1600	250	400000
Badagry	James	Sugar	4655	120	558600

Table 13.0

Data Subtotal

Let's assume that the above information has been entered in Excel. The first step is to arrange or group the data in the desired order. For the purpose of this exercise, we will sort the data in ascending order by column A (location) and then by column B (sales person). To do this, highlight the entire information and click Data, then Sort and follow the prompt. If you have questions on sorting or arranging information (see chapter 11).

After sorting, your data should appear thus:

	A	B	C	D	E	F	G
1	Town	Salesman	Product	Qty	Unit Cost	Total	
2	Badagry	Andrew	Butter	14,950.00	250.00	3,737,500.00	
3	Badagry	Andrew	Milk	7,866.00	45.00	353,970.00	
4	Badagry	Andrew	Sugar	2,500.00	120.00	300,000.00	
5	Badagry	James	Butter	5,900.00	250.00	1,475,000.00	
6	Badagry	James	Milk	1,400.00	45.00	63,000.00	
7	Badagry	James	Sugar	4,655.00	120.00	558,600.00	
8	Badagry	Stephen	Butter	4,500.00	250.00	1,125,000.00	
9	Badagry	Stephen	Milk	7,800.00	45.00	351,000.00	
10	Badagry	Stephen	Sugar	3,600.00	120.00	432,000.00	
11	Badagry	Thomas	Butter	1,600.00	250.00	400,000.00	
12	Badagry	Thomas	Milk	3,600.00	45.00	162,000.00	
13	Badagry	Thomas	Sugar	7,400.00	120.00	888,000.00	
14	Epe	Andrew	Butter	5,800.00	250.00	1,450,000.00	
15	Epe	Andrew	Milk	7,000.00	45.00	315,000.00	
16	Epe	Andrew	Sugar	4,590.00	120.00	550,800.00	
17	Epe	James	Butter	4,500.00	250.00	1,125,000.00	
18	Epe	James	Milk	5,000.00	45.00	225,000.00	
19	Epe	James	Sugar	9,000.00	120.00	1,080,000.00	
20	Epe	Stephen	Butter	9,000.00	250.00	2,250,000.00	
21	Epe	Stephen	Milk	7,500.00	45.00	337,500.00	
22	Epe	Stephen	Sugar	2,500.00	120.00	300,000.00	
23	Epe	Thomas	Butter	3,500.00	250.00	875,000.00	
24	Epe	Thomas	Milk	800.00	45.00	36,000.00	
25	Epe	Thomas	Sugar	7,000.00	120.00	840,000.00	
26	Lagos Island	Andrew	Butter	8,500.00	250.00	2,125,000.00	
27	Lagos Island	Andrew	Milk	7,000.00	45.00	315,000.00	
28	Lagos Island	Andrew	Sugar	56,000.00	120.00	6,720,000.00	
29	Lagos Island	James	Butter	8,000.00	250.00	2,000,000.00	
30	Lagos Island	James	Milk	6,000.00	45.00	270,000.00	
31	Lagos Island	James	Sugar	15,000.00	120.00	1,800,000.00	
32	Lagos Island	Stephen	Butter	8,500.00	250.00	2,125,000.00	
33	Lagos Island	Stephen	Milk	14,000.00	45.00	630,000.00	
34	Lagos Island	Stephen	Sugar	9,500.00	120.00	1,140,000.00	
35	Lagos Island	Thomas	Butter	9,500.00	250.00	2,375,000.00	
36	Lagos Island	Thomas	Milk	9,800.00	45.00	441,000.00	
37	Lagos Island	Thomas	Sugar	3,500.00	120.00	420,000.00	
38							

Fig 13.0

Next is to create the subtotal as earlier mentioned. Highlight the entire data and click Data, click Subtotal and the following screen will appear:

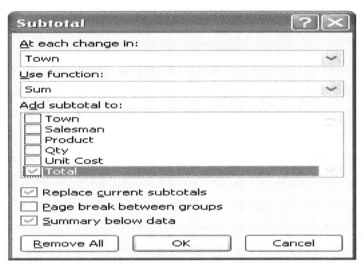

Fig 13.1

Under "At each change in:", select Town

Use function: click on Sum

Tick replace current subtotals

Summary below data: If this is not checked, your summary will be put on top of your data

Click ok to complete the subtotal and your data will appear thus:

1 2 3		A	B	C	D	E	F	G
·	8	Badagry	Stephen	Butter	4,500.00	250.00	1,125,000.00	
·	9	Badagry	Stephen	Milk	7,800.00	45.00	351,000.00	
·	10	Badagry	Stephen	Sugar	3,600.00	120.00	432,000.00	
·	11	Badagry	Thomas	Butter	1,600.00	250.00	400,000.00	
·	12	Badagry	Thomas	Milk	3,600.00	45.00	162,000.00	
·	13	Badagry	Thomas	Sugar	7,400.00	120.00	888,000.00	
−	14	Badagry Total					9,846,070.00	
·	15	Epe	Andrew	Butter	5,800.00	250.00	1,450,000.00	
·	16	Epe	Andrew	Milk	7,000.00	45.00	315,000.00	
·	17	Epe	Andrew	Sugar	4,590.00	120.00	550,800.00	
·	18	Epe	James	Butter	4,500.00	250.00	1,125,000.00	
·	19	Epe	James	Milk	5,000.00	45.00	225,000.00	
·	20	Epe	James	Sugar	9,000.00	120.00	1,080,000.00	
·	21	Epe	Stephen	Butter	9,000.00	250.00	2,250,000.00	
·	22	Epe	Stephen	Milk	7,500.00	45.00	337,500.00	
·	23	Epe	Stephen	Sugar	2,500.00	120.00	300,000.00	
·	24	Epe	Thomas	Butter	3,500.00	250.00	875,000.00	
·	25	Epe	Thomas	Milk	800.00	45.00	36,000.00	
·	26	Epe	Thomas	Sugar	7,000.00	120.00	840,000.00	
−	27	Epe Total					9,384,300.00	
·	28	Lagos Island	Andrew	Butter	8,500.00	250.00	2,125,000.00	
·	29	Lagos Island	Andrew	Milk	7,000.00	45.00	315,000.00	
·	30	Lagos Island	Andrew	Sugar	56,000.00	120.00	6,720,000.00	
·	31	Lagos Island	James	Butter	8,000.00	250.00	2,000,000.00	
·	32	Lagos Island	James	Milk	6,000.00	45.00	270,000.00	
·	33	Lagos Island	James	Sugar	15,000.00	120.00	1,800,000.00	
·	34	Lagos Island	Stephen	Butter	8,500.00	250.00	2,125,000.00	
·	35	Lagos Island	Stephen	Milk	14,000.00	45.00	630,000.00	
·	36	Lagos Island	Stephen	Sugar	9,500.00	120.00	1,140,000.00	
·	37	Lagos Island	Thomas	Butter	9,500.00	250.00	2,375,000.00	
·	38	Lagos Island	Thomas	Milk	9,800.00	45.00	441,000.00	
·	39	Lagos Island	Thomas	Sugar	3,500.00	120.00	420,000.00	
−	40	Lagos Island Total					20,361,000.00	
−	41	Grand Total					39,591,370.00	
	42							

Fig 13.2

Excel has automatically summarized the data and created an outline of the data. If you want to see only the summary, click either the (+) or (-) sign by the left to collapse or expand the information.

It is important to mention the fact that you can also create an inner subtotal, for instance, you want to know the total sales by sales person. Simply highlight the group you want to calculate subtotal on and click subtotal function again. Under "At each change of: ", pick salesman, click OK and a nested subtotal is created.

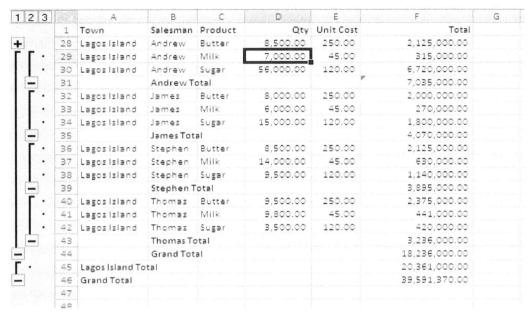

Fig 13.3

Expand/Collapse Subtotal

To expand subtotal, click on the + sign on the left and the system displays all the details of the rows under the group. To collapse, click on the negative sign on the left.

On the left hand (top corner), you have 123 see fig 13.3 above, 1 represents the ground total, 2 represents the sub-total of the next level while 3 represents the details. These numbers are generated based on the number of columns selected under "At each change in" earlier mentioned above.

Removing Subtotal

Removing subtotal is similar to the way it is created. Simply do the following:

- Highlight the subtotal you want to remove

- Select Data from the Main menu; click on Subtotal and the Subtotal Dialog Box earlier discussed appears.

- Click on Remove All

Your data will be returned automatically.

Notes:

14

Data Consolidation & Grouping

Introduction

Data consolidation in Microsoft Excel is the process of combining information from multiple ranges or worksheets into a single worksheet or range. Let's assume you have various reports coming from different sales region and you are giving the task of consolidating the result into a master data sheet, data consolidation will be a good tool to use for this type of project.

In order to get the best result from data consolidation, it is advisable to have all your columns properly labeled. In fact, the best practice is to prepare the worksheet template and send to all the users and if possible protect them from changing the column headings.

Let's look at the quarterly sales figures of XYZ Limited presented below. The company

	A	B	C	D	E	F
1			**XYZ LIMITED**			
2			SALES REPORT FOR YEAR 2009 -NORTHERN REGION			
3	Item	1st Quarter	2nd Quarter	3rd Quarter	4th Quarter	Total
4	Sugar	45,000	30,000	34,000	6,000	115,000
5	Rice	30,000	40,000	35,000	23,000	128,000
6	Beans	15,000	22,000	34,000	40,000	111,000
7	Corn	34,000	70,000	30,000	50,000	184,000
8	Millet	10,000	10,000	21,000	42,000	83,000
9	Bran	13,000	25,000	24,000	35,000	97,000
10	Total	147,000	197,000	178,000	196,000	718,000

operates in Northern and Southern parts of Nigeria with the following results:

Northern Region:

Table 14.0

Southern Region:

	A	B	C	D	E	F
1			**XYZ LIMITED**			
2		**SALES REPORT FOR YEAR 2009 -SOUTHERN REGION**				
3	Item	1st Quarter	2nd Quarter	3rd Quarter	4th Quarter	Total
4	Sugar	20,000	10,000	5,000	12,000	47,000
5	Rice	50,000	13,000	40,000	35,000	138,000
6	Beans	25,000	34,000	15,000	40,000	114,000
7	Corn	15,000	23,000	30,000	50,000	118,000
8	Millet	22,000	45,000	24,000	34,000	125,000
9	Bran	12,000	30,000	34,000	60,000	136,000
10	Total	144,000	155,000	148,000	231,000	678,000

Table 14.1

How to Consolidate Data

Data consolidation tool in Microsoft Excel is located under the Data Tools. Simply select Data from the Main menu, click on Consolidate and the Consolidate Dialog Box appears. We will discuss the dialog box as we consolidate the above sales reports.

To consolidate the two reports above, simply do the following:

a) Reproduce the above information on two different worksheets

b) Create the 3rd worksheet and copy rows 1 and 2 to the new worksheet. Change the content of row 2 to read "Consolidated Sales Report for the Year 2009"

c) Place your cursor on cell A3 to generate the summary.

d) Select Data from the standard or main menu and click on "Consolidate" from the Ribbon. The following dialog box will appear:

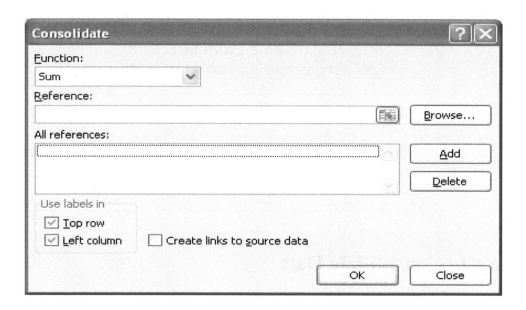

Fig 14.0

e) Select the Function to perform from the drop down menu by clicking on the arrow besides function. The functions include Sum, Count, Average, Max, Min, Product, Count Numbers, StdDev, StdDevp, Var and VarP

For this particular exercise, we will select Sum since we intend to add the sales figures from the two regions.

f) Under the Reference, click on the arrow by the side to collapse the dialog box and highlight cells A4:F10 from the first worksheet and click Add. Select cells A4:F10 from the second worksheet and click Add.

g) Under "Use Labels in", check both the Top row and the Left column. If you don't check both, your summary will not have row and column headings.

h) Do not check the box besides "Leave the Create links to source". The purpose of this is to create links to your source data. We will take a look at this in the next exercise

Your dialog box will look like this:

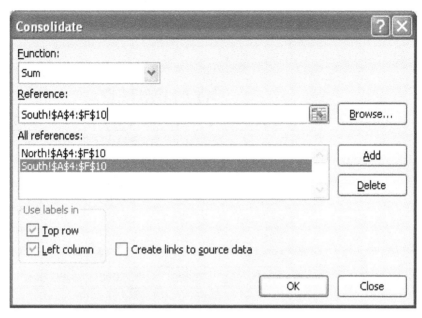

Fig 14.1

i) Click OK to complete the process.

j) Auto expand the columns, format it like the sheets above and your summary should look like this:

	A	B	C	D	E	F
1		XYZ LIMITED				
2		CONSOLIDATED SALES REPORT FOR YEAR 2009				
3		1st Quarter	2nd Quarter	3rd Quarter	4th Quarter	Total
4	Sugar	65,000	40,000	39,000	18,000	162,000
5	Rice	80,000	53,000	75,000	58,000	266,000
6	Beans	40,000	56,000	49,000	80,000	225,000
7	Corn	49,000	93,000	60,000	100,000	302,000
8	Millet	32,000	55,000	45,000	76,000	208,000
9	Bran	25,000	55,000	58,000	95,000	233,000
10	Total	291,000	352,000	326,000	427,000	1,396,000

Fig 14.2

If you want to make reference to your source data, create another sheet and repeat steps b to h above. Check the box besides "Create links to source data" and click OK to complete the process. Your summary looks like this:

Click here to show only the summary
Click here to show details of the entire summary

1 2		A	B	C	D	E	F	G
	1			XYZ LIMITED				
	2			CONSOLIDATED SALES REPORT FOR YEAR 2009				
	3			1st Quarter	2nd Quarter	3rd Quarter	4th Quarter	Total
+	6	Sugar		65,000	40,000	39,000	18,000	162,000
+	9	Rice		80,000	53,000	75,000	58,000	266,000
+	12	Beans		40,000	56,000	49,000	80,000	225,000
+	15	Corn		49,000	93,000	60,000	100,000	302,000
+	18	Millet		32,000	55,000	45,000	76,000	208,000
+	21	Bran		25,000	55,000	58,000	95,000	233,000
+	24	Total		291,000	352,000	326,000	427,000	1,396,000

Clikc on the **+** to expand and show details of a particular product

Fig 14.3

Note: It is possible to consolidate files but before you do that, make sure all the files are opened.

Grouping Data

Data grouping in Microsoft Excel is simply the process of tying range of selected cells together. It enables you to expand the group to show details or collapse the group to show the summary. Let's take a look at the summary of sales by the Northern Region earlier mentioned above. You may decide to group all the products together in such a way that if you collapse the group, only the total will show and if you expand it, all the products will show. You can group data in rows or in columns. Let group the sales report for the Northern Region:

a) Highlight rows 4 to 9

b) Select Data from the Main menu and click on Group. When the group dialog box appears, select Rows

c) To create another group, highlight rows 6 and 7 again and follow step (b) to complete the process. Your worksheet should look like this:

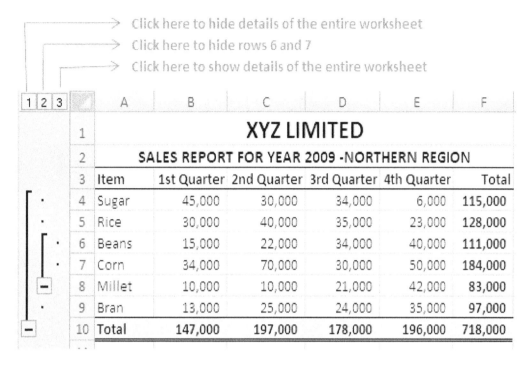

Fig 14.4

Note: Data Grouping will not affect your mathematical calculations.

Ungrouping Data

Data ungrouping enables you to ungroup your grouped data and return the worksheet to the original worksheet. Simply highlight the rows or columns you want to ungroup and click on Ungroup under the Data menu.

Notes:

15

What-If Analysis

Introduction

In a business environment, however certain a manager or an owner is, it is still practicable to consider various options or scenarios e.g. what happens if our output increases or decreases, what will be the effect of a slight increase in operating cost or what impact will a slight increase or decrease in selling price have on our profitability. What-If analysis in Microsoft Excel was designed to handle some of your what-if questions. There are three tools under what-if analysis:

1) Scenario Manager
2) The Goal Seek
3) The Data Table

Scenario Manager

Scenario Manager enables you to create and save different values in Microsoft Excel and switch between the values to generate automatic result. For example, the budget of XYZ for the first quarter of 2009 is presented below. XYZ Limited made the following assumptions when preparing the budget:

a) Selling price remains at $250 per unit and Unit Cost remains at $130.
b) XYZ anticipates 10% increase in quantity sold monthly
c) Salaries will increase by 2% monthly, rent and utility by 1% monthly while other costs increase by 3% monthly.

The big question is: What if those assumptions change?

	A	B	C	D	E	F	G
1				XYZ LIMITED			
3				BUDGET FOR Q1 OF 2009			
4			% increase	January	February	March	Total
5	Quantity Sold	10,000	10%	10,000	11,000	12,100	33,100
6	Selling Price	250	0%	250	250	250	
7	Unit Cost	130	0%	130	130	130	
9	Revenue			2,500,000	2,750,000	3,025,000	8,275,000
10	Variable Cost			1,300,000	1,430,000	1,573,000	4,303,000
11	Gross Profit			1,200,000	1,320,000	1,452,000	3,972,000
13	Administrative Charges						
14	Salaries	1,000,000	2%	1,000,000	1,020,000	1,040,400	3,060,400
15	Rent & Utility	50,000	1%	50,000	50,500	51,005	151,505
16	Others	250,000	3%	250,000	257,500	265,225	772,725
17	Total			1,300,000	1,328,000	1,356,630	3,984,630
19	Profit before Tax			(100,000)	(8,000)	95,370	(12,630)

Fig 15.0

The easiest way to know the impact is by creating scenarios. You can reproduce the above worksheet in Microsoft Excel.

Columns A to C: type the information as they appear. Formulas in other cells are:

D5   -   =B5

E5   -   =D5*$B5

F5   -   =E5*$B5

G5   -   =SUM(D5:F5)

Copy range D5:G5 to range D5:G7

Revenue = Quantity sold multiplied by selling price while Variable Cost = Quantity Sold multiplied by Unit Cost. Gross profit = Revenue less Variable Cost

Copy range D5:F5 to range D14:G16

Profit before tax = Gross profit less total administrative charges

Creating Scenario

Having reproduced the worksheet, let's now create scenarios and see the impact of changing the assumptions or variables by taking the following steps:

a) From the main menu, select Data, click on What-If Analysis and select Scenario Manager. The following dialog box appears

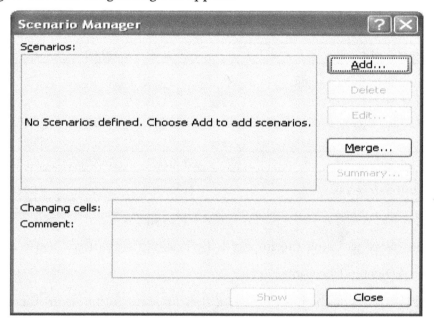

Fig 15.1

b) Click Add and the following dialog box appears:

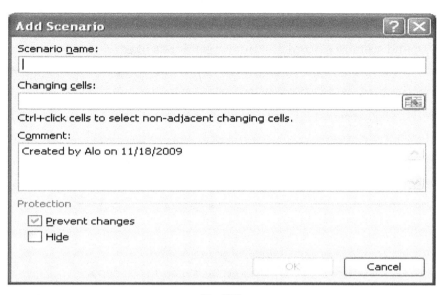

Fig 15.2

c) On the Scenario Name, type Scenario1

d) On the changing cells, highlight range B5:C7

e) Click OK and the following screen will appear

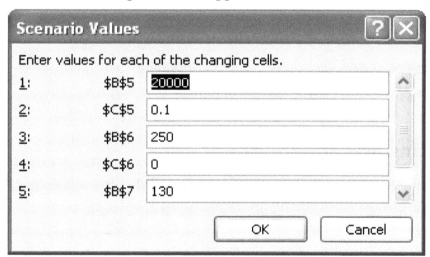

Fig 15.3

The dialog box shows all the values picked from the highlighted range. Click OK to accept the figures

f) Create Scenario2 and highlight range B14:C16 and accept the values. If you want to use the original values, create two additional scenarios with different names.

When you want to show the values, do not amend scenarios 1 and 2 but rather amend scenarios 3 and 4. Your screen looks like:

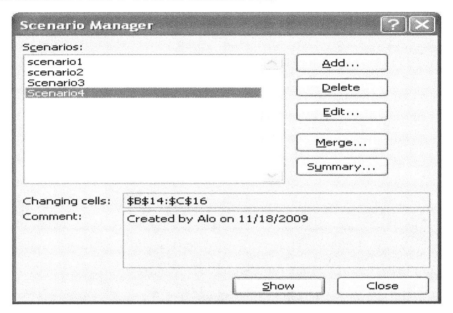

Fig 15.4

g) To see the effect of a slight change in any of the scenarios created, highlight the scenario and click Edit. Change the values and click Show. Your budget automatically reflects new set of figures.

Deleting Scenario

To delete scenario no longer required, click on What-If Analysis and select Scenario Manager, highlight the scenario to be deleted and click Delete

Merging Scenario

Merging Scenario is like copying scenario from other worksheets to your current worksheet. To merge scenario, go to the worksheet where you want merged scenario to reside and do the following:

a) Select Data from the Main menu and click on What-If Analysis

b) Select Scenario Manager

c) Click Merge and the following dialog box appears

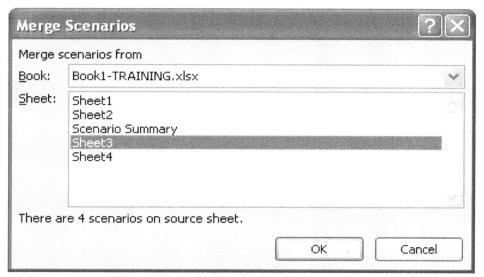

Fig 15.5

d) Under Book, select the workbook where you want to merge scenario from and all the worksheets in the workbook will appear

e) Select the worksheet that has the scenario

f) Click OK to complete the process.

Summarizing Scenarios

After you have created several scenarios in a worksheet, it is possible to forget the number of scenarios created or the changing cells. Summary of scenarios will display the changing cells, all the scenarios created and the current values of the cells. Let's summarize all the scenarios created in the above exercise:

a) Select Data from the Main menu and click on What-If Analysis

b) Click on Summary and the following screen will appear:

	Current Values:	scenario1	scenario2	Scenario3	Scenario4
Scenario Summary					
Changing Cells:					
$B$5	20,000	20,000	20,000	20,000	20,000
$C$5	10%	10%	10%	10%	10%
$B$6	300	250	300	300	300
$C$6	0%	0%	0%	0%	0%
$B$7	150	130	150	150	150
$C$7	0%	0%	0%	0%	0%
$C$8					
$B$14	1,000,000	1,000,000	1,000,000	1,000,000	1,000,000
$C$14	2%	2%	2%	2%	2%
$B$15	50,000	50,000	50,000	50,000	50,000
$C$15	1%	1%	1%	1%	1%
$B$16	250,000	250,000	250,000	250,000	250,000
$C$16	3%	3%	3%	3%	3%
Result Cells:					
$I$5					

Notes: Current Values column represents values of changing cells at time Scenario Summary Report was created. Changing cells for each scenario are highlighted in gray.

Fig 15.6

With this summary, you will be able to know the current values of all the scenarios and the changing cells.

Goal Seek

Goal Seek in Microsoft Excel is a tool that helps you determine the input required to achieve a desired goal. In a very simple term, you know your desired output and you have one of the variables but you are not sure of the second variable, e.g. 900 + something equals 1899. What is the something to be added to 900 to get 1899? Goal Seek will help you determine the missing figure. Let's handle the simple illustration in Excel by taking the following steps:

a) Type Input1 in cell A1 and type 900 in cell B1

b) Leave row 2 blank and type Required Output in cell A3

c) Type the formula =B1+B2 in cell B3. Your initial screen looks like this:

	A	B
1	Input 1	900
2		
3	Required Output	900

Fig 15.7

d) Select Data from the Main menu and click on What-If Analysis, select Goal Seek and the Goal Seek dialog box appears

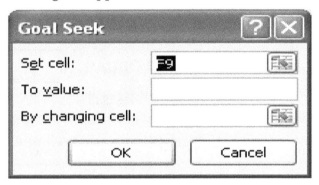

Fig 15.8

There are three fields to be completed.

1) **Set Cell**: This represents your required output which is cell B3 in this case. This cell must contain formula for the Goal Seek to work. The formula in cell B3 tells Excel to add cells B1 and B2 together.

2) **To Value**: This represents your goal or output which in this case is 1899. Type in 1899 in that field

3) **By Changing Cell**: This is the cell where the missing figure should be placed which in this case is cell B2.

After completing the fields, your screen should look like this:

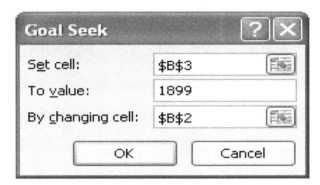

Fig 15.9

e) Click OK to complete the process and your screen will look like this:

	A	B
1	Input 1	900
2		999
3	Required Output	1899

Fig 15.10

This is a very simple illustration of Goal seek. You can however use it to solve complex problem. Just be sure you have the correct formula in the cell you are using as the Set Cell and your result will be reliable. Examples of what you can use Goal Seek to achieve include:

What will be our selling price or cost price to achieve a targeted profit?

What interest rate do I use to achieve a monthly loan repayment of a specified amount and many more?

Data Table

Data Table is one of the analyzing tools under What-If Analysis that enables you consider several outcome of a maximum of two inputs. When using Scenario Manager for instance, you can have as many as 32 inputs per scenario but you can create as many scenarios as possible. In the case of Data Table, you can have a maximum of 2 inputs with as many outputs as possible. There are two types of data table:

a) One-Way Data Table

In a one-way Data Table, you only have one input which can either be in column or row. You will be determining the output based on a change in only one variable. For instance, in a business environment, you might want to know the profit based on the quantities sold between 7500 units and 15000 units. In this case, the only input is quantity. Once you have entered your various formulas in the relevant cells, all you need is to enter the quantities either in columns or row and Data Table automatically fills the cells.

Let's demonstrate this with the information below:

XYZ Limited has a single product line with the following information:

Selling Price $60, Variable Unit Cost $35. XYZ sold 6500 unit in 2009 and is considering his profit for the coming year. XYZ has a fixed cost of $120,000 irrespective of quantity sold and also incurs advertising cost of $30000 if quantity sold falls below 7500 units but advert cost increases to $50000 once sales increase beyond 7500 units. What will be the profit of XYZ between 6000 and 9000 units at every additional sale of 500 units?

Let's prepare a format for the above information. I will only mention those cells with formula which are:

Revenue C7 and C14 - =C3*C4, Total Variable Cost C8 and D14 - =C3*C5

Fixed Cost C9 and E14 - =if(C3<=6000,30000,50000)

Profit/(Loss) C11 and G14 - =C7-sum(C8:C10).

You can start the quantity from C15 and enter the formula C15+500 in cell C16. Copy the formula down until you get to 9000. Your worksheet should look like the one below:

	A	B	C	D	E	F	G
1			XYZ LIMITED				
2			BUDGET FOR 2010				
3		Qty Sold	6,500				
4		Selling Price	60				
5		Variable unit cost	35				
7		Revenue	390,000				
8		Total Variable Cost	227,500				
9		Fixed Cost	30,000				
10		Other Cost	120,000				
11		Profit/(Loss)	12,500				
13			Revenue	Variable Cost	Fixed Cost	Other Cost	Profit
14	Quantity Sold		390,000	227,500	30,000	120,000	12,500
15		6,000					
16		6,500					
17		7,000					
18		7,500					
19		8,000					
20		8,500					
21		9,000					

Fig 15.11

If you take note of the above, we have not filled range C15 to G21. The Data Table tool will take care of that. It is however important to ensure that you have the correct formulas in cells C14 to G14 because the Data Table will use the formulas to generate figures for the cells below them. Let's generate the data by taking the following steps:

a) Highlight range B14 to G21

b) Select Data from the main menu, click on What-If Analysis and select Data Table. The Data Table dialog box appears;

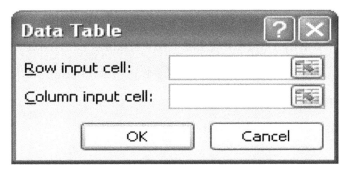

Fig 15.12

c) We are using a single input data table. Your row input cell should be left blank while your column input cell should read cell C3.

d) Once you click OK, Microsoft Excel will fill the Data Table and your screen will look like this:

	A	B	C	D	E	F	G
1			XYZ LIMITED				
2			BUDGET FOR 2010				
3		Qty Sold	6,500				
4		Selling Price	60				
5		Variable unit cost	35				
7		Revenue	390,000				
8		Total Variable Cost	227,500				
9		Fixed Cost	30,000				
10		Other Cost	120,000				
11		Profit/(Loss)	12,500				
13			Revenue	Variable Cost	Fixed Cost	Other Cost	Profit
14	Quantity Sold		390,000	227,500	30,000	120,000	12,500
15		6,000	360,000	210,000	30,000	120,000	-
16		6,500	390,000	227,500	30,000	120,000	12,500
17		7,000	420,000	245,000	30,000	120,000	25,000
18		7,500	450,000	262,500	50,000	120,000	17,500
19		8,000	480,000	280,000	50,000	120,000	30,000
20		8,500	510,000	297,500	50,000	120,000	42,500
21		9,000	540,000	315,000	50,000	120,000	55,000

Fig 15.13

b) Two-Way Data Table

The major difference between a one-way Data Table and a two-way Data Table is the fact that a two-way Data Table has two variables i.e. two inputs. In the illustration above, let's assume we are considering both the change in quantity sold as well as the change in unit variable cost, a two-way Data Table will be more ideal. We will illustrate this using the same data above.

a) Reorganize the data of XYZ Limited as follows:

	A	B	C	D	E	F	G
1			XYZ LIMITED				
2			BUDGET FOR 2010				
3		Qty Sold	6,500				
4		Selling Price	60				
5		Variable unit cost	35				
7		Revenue	390,000				
8		Total Variable Cost	227,500				
9		Fixed Cost	30,000				
10		Other Cost	120,000				
11		Profit/(Loss)	12,500				
13					Variable Cost -->		
14	Quantity Sold	12,500	35	37	40	45	50
15		6,000					
16		6,500					
17		7,000					
18		7,500					
19		8,000					
20		8,500					
21		9,000					

Fig 15.14

Cells C14 to G14 contain the various variable costs to be considered while cells B15 to B21 relate to the quantities sold. I have highlighted cell B14 in red because it picks the formula for our profit. It is not quantity but the formula for profit. Simply type =C11 in cell B14.

b) Highlight range B14 to G21

c) Select Data from the Main menu, click on What-If Analysis and select Data Table

d) When the Data Table dialog box appears, click cell C5 as your Row Input and cell C3 as your Column Input. Your dialog box should look like this:

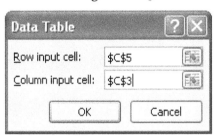

Fig 15.15

e) Click OK to complete the process. Your Data Table should look like the one below:

	A	B	C	D	E	F	G
1			XYZ LIMITED				
2			BUDGET FOR 2010				
3		Qty Sold	6,500				
4		Selling Price	60				
5		Variable unit cost	35				
7		Revenue	390,000				
8		Total Variable Cost	227,500				
9		Fixed Cost	30,000				
10		Other Cost	120,000				
11		Profit/(Loss)	12,500				
13				Variable Cost -->			
14	Quantity Sold	12,500	35	37	40	45	50
15		6,000	-	(12,000)	(30,000)	(60,000)	(90,000)
16		6,500	12,500	(500)	(20,000)	(52,500)	(85,000)
17		7,000	25,000	11,000	(10,000)	(45,000)	(80,000)
18		7,500	17,500	2,500	(20,000)	(57,500)	(95,000)
19		8,000	30,000	14,000	(10,000)	(50,000)	(90,000)
20		8,500	42,500	25,500	-	(42,500)	(85,000)
21		9,000	55,000	37,000	10,000	(35,000)	(80,000)

Fig 15.16

From the table above, your profit will be zero if you sell 6000 units at a variable cost of $35 or if you sell 8500 unit at a variable cost of $40.

Notes:

16

Excel Tables

You will cover:

- *Introduction*
- *Creating Excel Table*

Introduction

Managing and analyzing group of related data can be a major challenge where you have data running into columns and rows. In such situations, organizing or sorting could be confusing. With Excel Table function, you can manage your data better with a high degree of efficiency. Once your data has been converted to Table, sorting, formatting summarizing and working with the data becomes easier.

How to Create a Table

Creating a Table in Excel involves the following:

a) Highlight the data you want to convert into a Table. This can be either existing data or even range of blank cells

b) Select Insert from the Main Menu and click on Table Table . The Table dialog box appears as follows:

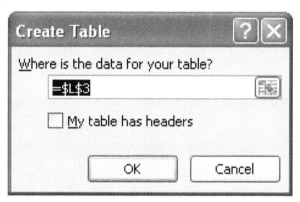

Fig 16.0

c) If your data has a row you intend to use as the header or column label, tick the box besides "My table has headers"

d) Click OK to complete the process

Once the process is complete, a new menu titled "Table Tools" appears and if you click the Design under the table tools, various table related icons arranged in groups will appear on the Ribbon:

- **Properties**:

Under Properties, you can change the name of the table from the generic name assigned by Excel to a more meaningful name of your choice by simply typing a new name under Table Name. You can also resize the table either by extending the range to cover more cells or reducing the range. To do this, simply click on Resize Table.

- **Tools**:

Under the Tools, you can summarize with PivotTable, remove Duplicate rows or even convert the table back to normal range of cells without losing information.

- **External Table Data**:

The External Table Data gives you the opportunity to export table to a shared point where your table can be updated by other users. The refresh icon enables you to update the data while the unlink cuts off connection to the data by other users.

- **Table Style Options**:

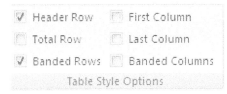

Under the Table Style Options, you will be able to add or remove Header Row, Total Row, Banded Rows, First Column, Last Column and Banded Column

- **Table Style Options**:

We also have Table Styles where you can select automatic styles for your table. We will now try and insert Data Table using one of our previous worksheets. Below is the sales report from the Southern part of the country:

	A	B	C	D	E
1	**XYZ LIMITED**				
2	**SALES REPORT FOR YEAR 2009 -SOUTHERN REGION**				
3	Item	1st Quarter	2nd Quarter	3rd Quarter	4th Quarter
4	Sugar	20,000	10,000	5,000	12,000
5	Rice	50,000	13,000	40,000	35,000
6	Beans	25,000	34,000	15,000	40,000
7	Corn	15,000	23,000	30,000	50,000
8	Millet	22,000	45,000	24,000	34,000
9	Bran	12,000	30,000	34,000	60,000

Fig 16.1

As you can see, the above information is presently not a Data Table but can be converted to Data Table. To convert the information to Data Table, follow the steps below:

a) Highlight range A3 to E9

b) Select Insert from the Main menu and click on Table. The Create Table dialog box appears.

c) Since we have header row which in this case is row 3, check the box besides "My Table has Header"

d) Click OK to complete the process. Your table looks like the one below:

	A	B	C	D	E
1			XYZ LIMITED		
2		SALES REPORT FOR YEAR 2009 -SOUTHERN REGION			
3	Item ▼	1st Quart ▼	2nd Quart ▼	3rd Quart ▼	4th Quart ▼
4	Sugar	20,000	10,000	5,000	12,000
5	Rice	50,000	13,000	40,000	35,000
6	Beans	25,000	34,000	15,000	40,000
7	Corn	15,000	23,000	30,000	50,000
8	Millet	22,000	45,000	24,000	34,000
9	Bran	12,000	30,000	34,000	60,000

Fig 16.2

e) Place your cursor on cell F4 and type the formula =SUM(B4:E4). Excel automatically converts the formula to:

=SUM(Table1[[#This Row],[1st Quarter]:[4th Quarter]])

It also complete the remaining rows in the column

f) Place your cursor on cell B10 and type the formula =SUM(B4:B9). Excel automatically converts the formula to: =SUM([1st Quarter]) with a drop down arrow at the bottom.

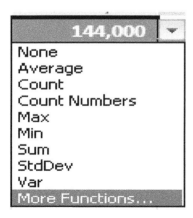

You can click on any of those items discussed under the Design menu and see the effect on the table.

17

PivotTable Reports

You will cover:

- *Introduction*
- *PivotTable with Single Range*
- *PivotTable with Multiple Worksheets*
- *PivotChart*

Introduction

If you really want to query, analyze and summarize large amount of data with ability to present it in different ways, you need to grasp the idea of PivotTable function, With PivotTable, you can use various criteria to summarize or analyze your data with ease. PivotTable can be used to analyze single worksheet or range or multiple worksheets or several ranges. Both of them are similar to some extent but the differences will be analyzed when we handle multiple worksheets.

PIVOTTABLE FOR SINGLE RANGE

The PivotTable to cover single range can be accessed by simply clicking the Insert Menu as shown below:

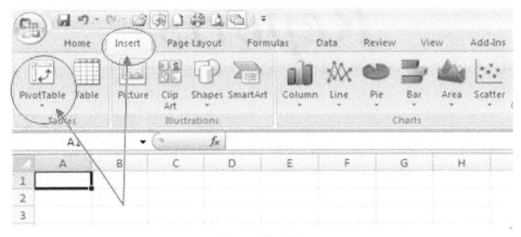

Fig 17.0

Once you click the PivotTable, a dialog box will appear that will guide you through the whole process. Let's make an attempt to summarize the data below. When using a PivotTable, it is not compulsory to sort your data but if you decide to do it, all is well. In order to summarize the data, do the following:

1) Select sheet1 and highlight range A1 to F25

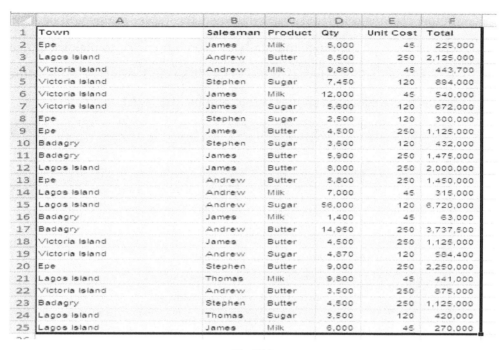

	A	B	C	D	E	F
1	Town	Salesman	Product	Qty	Unit Cost	Total
2	Epe	James	Milk	5,000	45	225,000
3	Lagos Island	Andrew	Butter	8,500	250	2,125,000
4	Victoria Island	Andrew	Milk	9,860	45	443,700
5	Victoria Island	Stephen	Sugar	7,450	120	894,000
6	Victoria Island	James	Milk	12,000	45	540,000
7	Victoria Island	James	Sugar	5,600	120	672,000
8	Epe	Stephen	Sugar	2,500	120	300,000
9	Epe	James	Butter	4,500	250	1,125,000
10	Badagry	Stephen	Sugar	3,600	120	432,000
11	Badagry	James	Butter	5,900	250	1,475,000
12	Lagos Island	James	Butter	8,000	250	2,000,000
13	Epe	Andrew	Butter	5,800	250	1,450,000
14	Lagos Island	Andrew	Milk	7,000	45	315,000
15	Lagos Island	Andrew	Sugar	56,000	120	6,720,000
16	Badagry	James	Milk	1,400	45	63,000
17	Badagry	Andrew	Butter	14,950	250	3,737,500
18	Victoria Island	James	Butter	4,500	250	1,125,000
19	Victoria Island	Andrew	Sugar	4,870	120	584,400
20	Epe	Stephen	Butter	9,000	250	2,250,000
21	Lagos Island	Thomas	Milk	9,800	45	441,000
22	Victoria Island	Andrew	Butter	3,500	250	875,000
23	Badagry	Stephen	Butter	4,500	250	1,125,000
24	Lagos Island	Thomas	Sugar	3,500	120	420,000
25	Lagos Island	James	Milk	6,000	45	270,000

Fig 17.1

2) Select Insert and click on PivotTable. The following dialog box will appear:

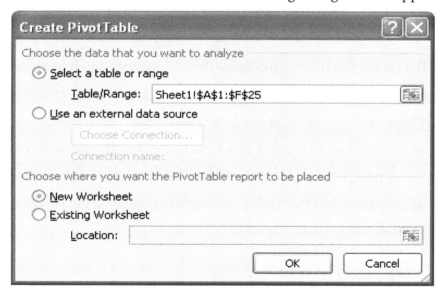

Fig 17.2

Note that in the above dialog box, the system has automatically selected Sheet1!$A$1:$F$25. This is simply because you have highlighted the range before clicking on PivotTable; otherwise, the Table/Range will be blank and you can either type the range manually or use your cursor to pick the range.

If you are using external data, click "Use and external data source" and a connection dialog box shown below will be displayed:

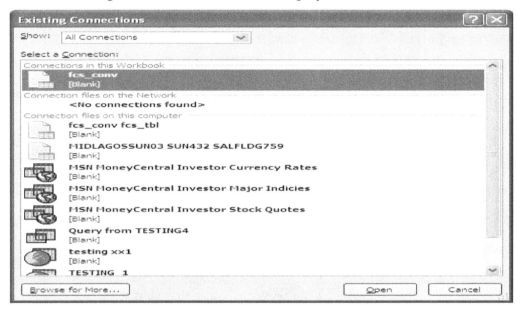

Fig 17.3

The connection dialog box shows the various files you have accessed in the past either on your current workbook, the network or your computer.

3) Choose where you want the PivotTable report to be placed: You can select a new Worksheet or existing Worksheet. For the purpose of this exercise, we will use a new Worksheet. Select New Worksheet and click ok to accept your selections. A new PivotTable Tool with two optional menu will appear:

   a) PivotTable Tools – Options

   b) PivotTable Tools – Design

PivotTable Tools Options:

Several items have been group under the options to make them easily accessible to users. Following are the groups and item under each of them:

a)   Options: This is where you can change the PivotTable Name.

Apart from this, it has the following four additional tabs:

- **Layout & Format:** where you can set your layout and format of the PivotTable output. Under layout, you can merge cells or center cells with label. You can also show the order of display e.g. "down, then over" or "over, then down". Under format, you may decide to show error value, designate specific character for blank cells, auto-fit column width and preserve cell formatting upon update.

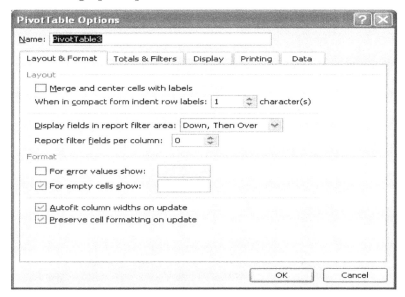

Fig 17.4

- Totals & Filters: You can set whether to show grand totals in rows or columns. You can also enable multiple filters per field and set your sorting parameter.

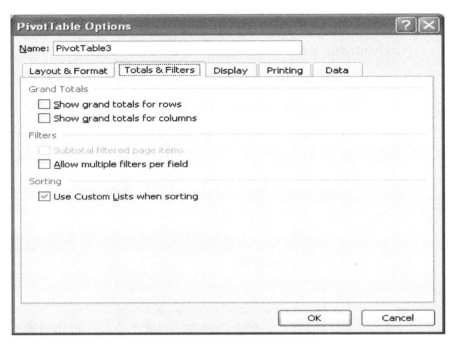

Fig 17.5

- Display: This assist you to set what you want to see on the PivotTable such as expand/collapse button, tooltips, field captions, filter drop downs, dragging of fields, order of sorting, etc.

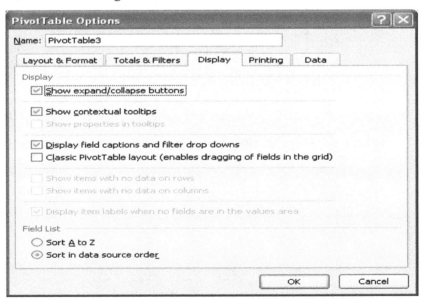

Fig 17.6

- Printing: This is to enable you set print parameters

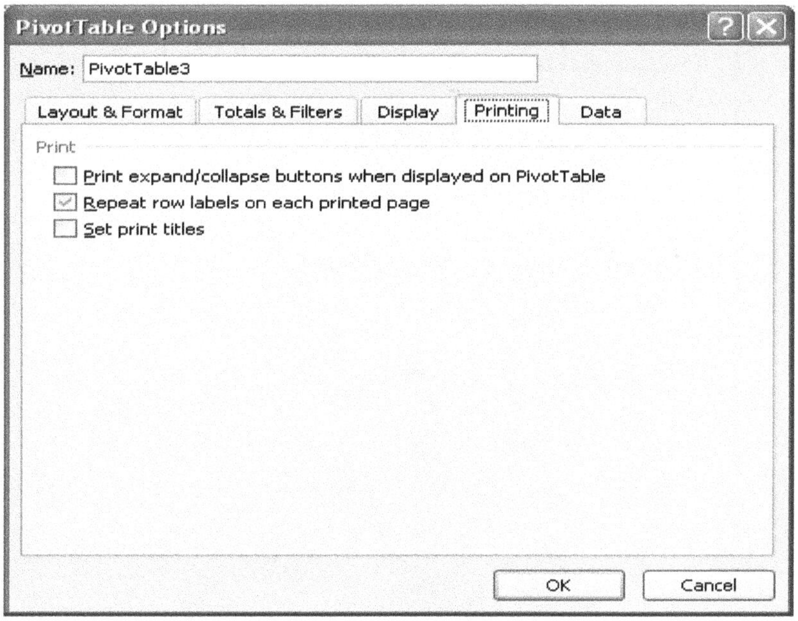

Fig 17.7

- Data: Here, you will tell the system whether to save source data with the file, enable show details and whether you want to refresh data when opening the file. If you enable details, you can double click on any of the PivotTable result and the details will be automatically generated.

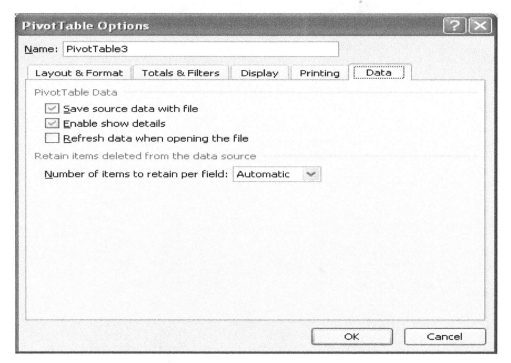

Fig 17.8

b) **Active Field**: Under this group, you have the following:

- Active Field: This displays the particular field your cursor is on the PivotTable.

- Field Setting: Under this, we have Subtotals & Filters where you can set the parameters whether you want your subtotals to be automatic, none or customs. You can also include or exclude new items in manual filter.

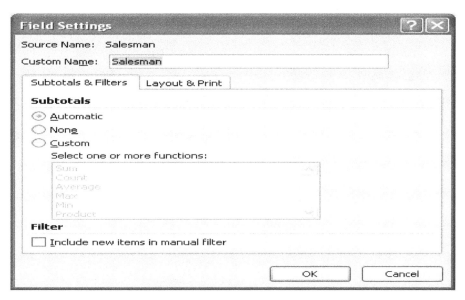

Fig 17.9

- Next is the Layout & Print where you can set your parameters for the layout i.e. how you want the PivotTable to appear. You can play with any of them to familiarize yourself with the various options.

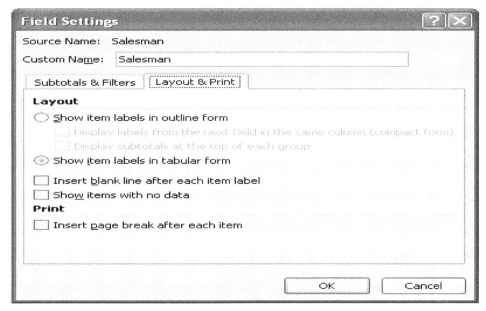

Fig 17.10

- Expand Entire Field: This enables you to add additional fields to your PivotTable Report.

- Collapse Entire Field: This enables you to collapse the field

c) **Group:** Here you can group and ungroup your data based on your desired selections.

d) **Sort:** You can sort your PivotTable in any order of preference i.e. manual sorting or automatic sorting. With manual sorting, you can just drag any of the items and your PivotTable will be sorted accordingly. You may decide to sort in either ascending or descending order as well.

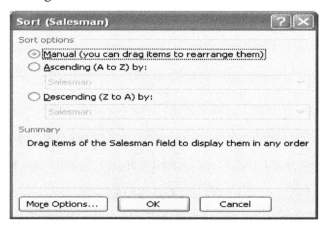

Fig 17.11

We have more options under sorting where you can select your sort key order (see below):

Fig 17.12

e) **Data**: This is where you can refresh your PivotTable to incorporate changes made to the original data source. This can also be achieved by doing the following:

- Right-click inside the PivotTable
- Click Refresh from the list of menu that appears.

You can also change your data source in this group. Click on change data source and the following dialog box will appear for you to either select the range of data or use external data source:

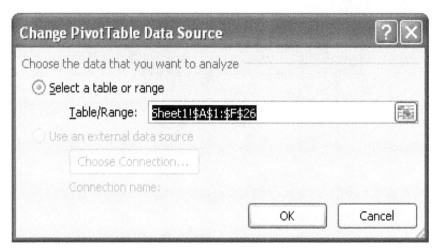

Fig 17.13

f)   **Actions**: There are three options under Actions vis:

   • Clear: You can clear the entire PivotTable or the Filter

   • Select: When you click Select, the following screen appears for you to select "label and values", values, labels or the entire PivotTable

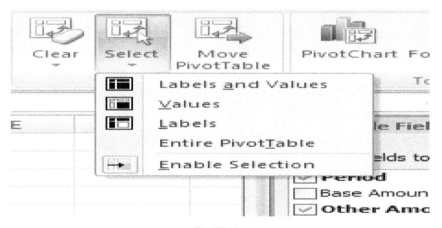

Fig 17.14

   • Move PivotTable: This enables you to move the PivotTable from one location to the other. You can choose a new worksheet or existing worksheet.

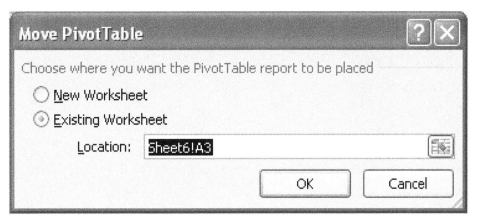

Fig 17.15

g)   Tools: Under the tools, we have the following:

- **PivotChart**: Once you click on this, a chart is automatically generated for the PivotTable (see page 217).

- **Formulas:** This has 4 other options under it.

   1)   Calculated Field: This enables you to insert additional column for calculation. This could be average, formula resulting from manipulation of fields from the PivotTable, etc. Once clicked, the following dialog box appears:

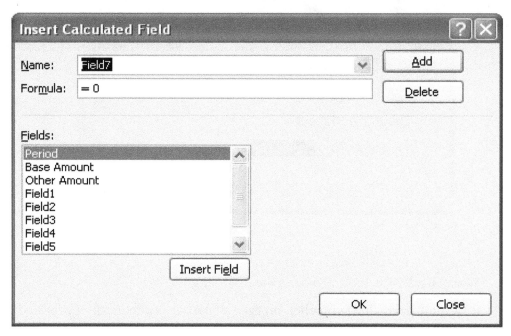

Fig 17.16

Name: Indicates the description or the title of the new field you are trying to insert

Formula: The formula for the field. This can also be number, combination of fields, etc. If you enter a new field, the Add button appears; otherwise, the Add button will change to Modify if you pick an existing field from the drop down box. You can hit the Delete button at any time to delete the formula. If you intend to use the result of a field, click insert field and the field will appear in the formula bar. Click OK to complete your entries. The new field or column will appear on the PivotTable.

2) Solve Order: This is applicable where you have calculated items. It enables you to specify the order of calculation.

3) List Formulas: This creates a worksheet and lists all the formulas in the calculated field (see sample below).

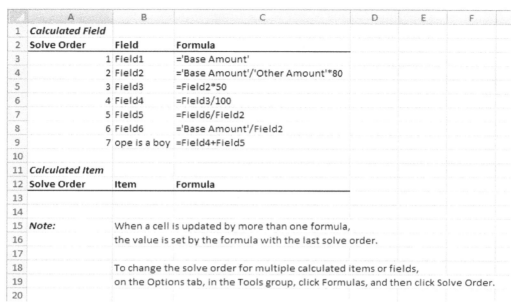

	A	B	C	D	E	F
1	*Calculated Field*					
2	Solve Order	Field	Formula			
3		1 Field1	='Base Amount'			
4		2 Field2	='Base Amount'/'Other Amount'*80			
5		3 Field3	=Field2*50			
6		4 Field4	=Field3/100			
7		5 Field5	=Field6/Field2			
8		6 Field6	='Base Amount'/Field2			
9		7 ope is a boy	=Field4+Field5			
10						
11	*Calculated Item*					
12	Solve Order	Item	Formula			
13						
14						
15	*Note:*		When a cell is updated by more than one formula,			
16			the value is set by the formula with the last solve order.			
17						
18			To change the solve order for multiple calculated items or fields,			
19			on the Options tab, in the Tools group, click Formulas, and then click Solve Order.			
20						

Fig 17.17

h)   Show/Hide: This has three other items that can be useful when working with PivotTable which are:

- **Field List:** This hides or displays all the relevant fields of the PivotTable. The following screen will display if the Field List icon is highlighted:

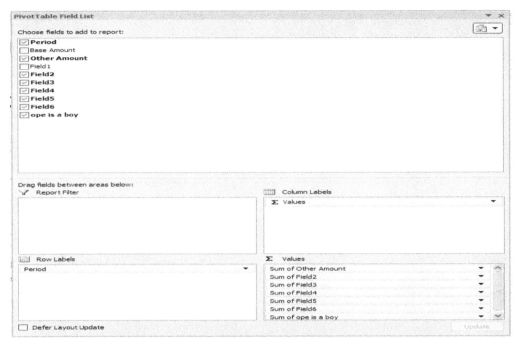

Fig 17.18

The upper part named PivotTable Field List displays all the fields of the PivotTable. Only selected fields in this part will appear on the PivotTable Report

The next section is divided into various sections depending on what you have selected, there are four parts:

a) Report Filter: This enables you to create filter at the report level. For example, let's assume we are going to run our sales report by town, we can drag the town to the report filter area. You will then be able to generate the PivotTable for each town separately. The best way to understand the behavior of a PivotTable is to try some of this.

b) Row Labels: Fields in this section will determine how subtotals are generated. Transactions in the columns are converted to rows and used to summarize the other fields. As you drag in more fields, you have more nested subtotals.

c) Column Labels: Fields in this section of the PivotTable Field List determine the horizontal grouping of your data. For instance, if you drag a column that has several rows to this field, row entries will be transposed to column headings for the purpose of summarizing your data.

d)   Values: This determines the mathematical functions you want to perform on the fields e.g. sum of total, count, etc.

Once you have dragged your information to the field, a box with an arrow appears by the right where you can modify your settings, move, delete or edit your fields.

- +/- Button: This hides or displays buttons that will enable you to expand or collapse items on a PivotTable Report

- Field Header: This displays or hides the field header in the PivotTable report.

PivotTable Tools Design:

After we have completed creating the PivotTable, we can make it more readable and attractive with the Design Tools. These tools are group into Layout, PivotTable Style Options and PivotTable Styles to make it easier to work with (see diagram below)

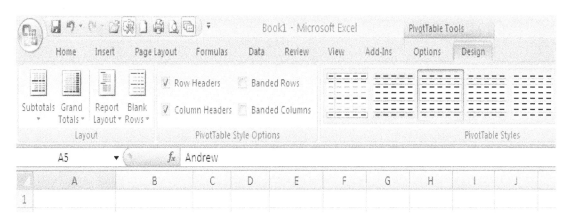

Fig 17.19

a)   **Layout**: Under the Layout, the following options are available:

- Subtotals: There are three options under the Subtotals:

    1. Do not show Subtotals: This will hide all subtotals from your PivotTable Report

2. Show all Subtotals at Bottom of Group: This shows subtotals at the bottom of each group

3. Show all Subtotals at Top of Group: Shows subtotals on top instead of the bottom.

- Grand Totals: There are four options for Grand Totals:

  1. Off For Rows and Columns

  2. On for Rows and Columns

  3. On for Rows only

  4. On for Columns only

- Report Layout: This enables you to show your PivotTable Report in compact, outline or tabular form.

b) **PivotTable Style Options**: Under the Style Options, you may decide to show the Row Header, the Column Header, Branded Rows or Branded Columns

c) **PivotTable Styles**: Under the Styles, you can pick and format of your choice and your PivotTable will be formatted automatically.

PIVOTTABLE FOR MULTIPLE WORKSHEETS

As earlier mentioned, there is no major difference between PivotTable with single range and multiple worksheets other than the fact that you can select multiple worksheets at the same time. You can only access this with the combination of keys unlike the conventional PivotTable that you can access through the Insert Menu. To access PivotTable with multiple worksheets, press the following sequence of keys:

Alt + D + P

The following screen will appear:

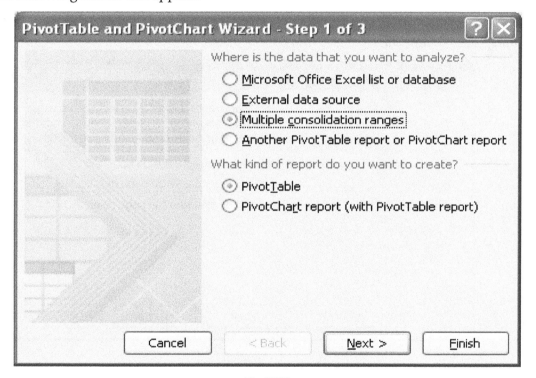

Fig 17.20

There are four options under "Where is the data that you want to analyze?":

1) Microsoft Office Excel list of database: This is similar to the conventional PivotTable earlier treated above

2) External data source: This is also similar to the using external data source earlier discussed.

3) Multiple consolidation ranges: This enables you to highlight ranges from various worksheets to aid consolidation. This is a wonderful tool that can save you considerable amount of time when consolidating data. It is pertinent to arrange your data in an organized manner to get the best out of this.

4) Another PivotTable Report or PivotChart Report: This will basically allow you to generate your report from another PivotTable or PivotChart Report earlier generated.

We are now going to concentrate on Multiple Consolidation Ranges. From figure 17.20 above, check the box beside Multiple consolidation Ranges and the following dialog box will appear:

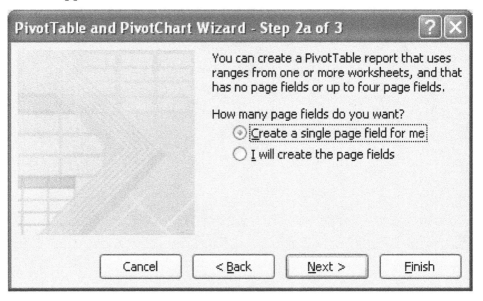

Fig 17.21

This is step 2a where you can decide whether to create a single page field or multiple page fields. If you select a single page field, Excel automatically creates the page field without asking you about page field in step 2b. If you select "Create a single page field for me", the following screen (step 2b) appears:

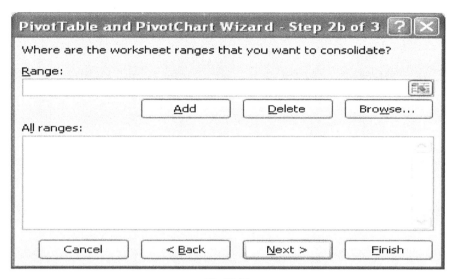

Fig 17.22

You can select multiple ranges from either a single worksheet or various worksheets. Simply put your cursor inside Range or click the arrow beside it to minimize the screen. Highlight the range and click Add and the selected range appears under "All ranges". Do that for all the data you intend to consolidate and go to the next step which is step 3 of 3.

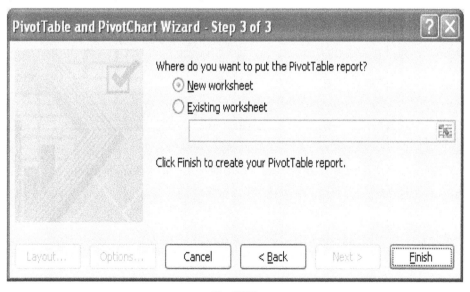

Fig 17.23

Decide whether you want to put the PivotTable report in a new worksheet or an existing worksheet. Click "Finish" and follow all other steps earlier discussed under the Single PivotTable Report.

If you however select "I will create the Page Fields" under step 2a above, the screen that you will see under step 2b will be slightly different from the one earlier discussed because of the page fields. You can create up to a maximum of 4 page fields for your consolidated data.

Fig 17.24

Select all the ranges as earlier discussed under step 2b above.

Page Field

Page Field is similar to the Report Filter under the conventional PivotTable Report. It means you can filter by each item under each page field. Let's look at a situation where you have an annual information arranged monthly in various tabs say January, February, March, etc. and your intention is to consolidate all the information on a single sheet. You may decide to have about 3 page fields namely: Monthly, Quarterly and Biannually. This means that if you select all months on page 1, select a specific quarter on page 2, you will have total of the quarter selected. Let's use the information below to create a multiple ranges PivotTable:

A company sells 4 products with following price and cost information:

Product	Unit Selling Price	Unit Cost Price
N	N	
Milk	50	45
Sugar	45	40
Tea	60	50
Butter	750	700

During the year, the following items were sold:

	Jan	Feb	Mar	Apr	May	Jun	Jul	Aug	Sep	Oct	Nov	Dec
Milk	50	80	100	25	100	50	85	40	250	68	45	60
Sugar	1	5	25	2	30	6	6	55	45	15	25	50
Tea	75	90	900	100	150	56	90	35	68	80	100	290
Butter	3	5	30	4	45	9	60	10	3	9	20	60
Bread	70	66	450	40	98	400	140	77	20	35	88	200

Table 17.0

Use the information above to determine Sales, Cost of Sales and the Margin for each month on different sheets. The table for each sheet should look like this:

	A	B	C	D	E	F	G	H
1	January							
2	Product	Qty	USP	UCP	Sales	Cost	Margin	
3	Milk	50	50	45	2,500	2,250	250	
4	Sugar	1	45	40	45	40	5	
5	Tea	75	60	50	4,500	3,750	750	
6	Butter	3	750	700	2,250	2,100	150	
7	Bread	70	120	110	8,400	7,700	700	
8	Total				17,695	15,840	1,855	
9								

Fig 17.25

Repeat the above for each month for the rest of the year. At the end, you will have about 12 different sheets for the year. We will make an attempt to consolidate the 12 worksheets using PivotTable Report. We will assume that your monthly data covers cells A1 to G8 in each of the twelve sheets. Let's create a PivotTable report with multiple ranges and multiple Page Fields by following the steps below:

1. Press Alt + D and touch P to display the PivotTable wizard
2. Select "Multiple Consolidated Ranges" and PivotTable Report and click Next. This will take you to Step 2a
3. Select "I will create the page fields" and click Next to take you to step 2b
4. Click inside "Range" in step 2b and select the range by highlighting cells A2:G7 in the first worksheet
5. Click "Add" and the following appears under All Ranges: 'Sheet1'!$A$2:$G$7
6. Repeat steps 4 and 5 until you have selected all the ranges in the twelve worksheets.
7. Select 3 under "How many page fields do you want?" and your screen should look like this

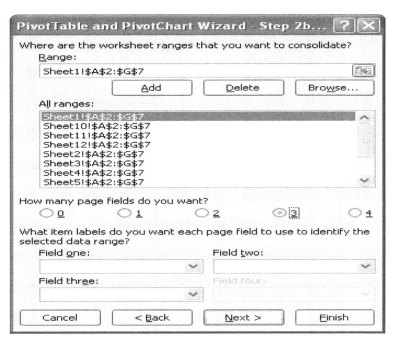

Fig 17.26

8. Highlight the cell that corresponds with your data for January. Type January inside Field one, type 1st Quarter inside Field two and type 1st Half inside field three. Highlight February data and type February in Field one, 1st Quarter in field two and 1st Half in Field three. Repeat same for March data. When you get to April data, change Field two to 2nd Quarter and repeat 1st Half in Field three. Repeat same for May and June. When you highlight July, type July in Field one, 3rd Quarter in Field two and 2nd Half in Field three and repeat same for August and September. When you highlight October, type October in Field one, 3rd Quarter in Field two and 2nd Half in Field three. Repeat same for November and December and your screen should be similar to this:

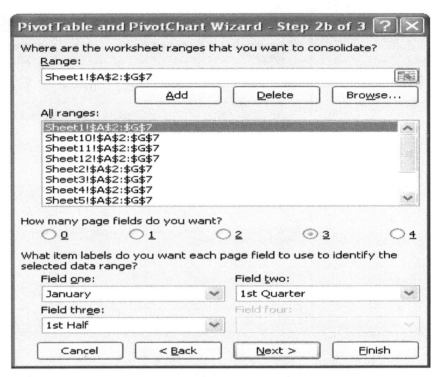

Fig 17.27

9. Click Next to go to Step 3. Select where you like your report to be and click Finish. Your PivotTable Report should look like this:

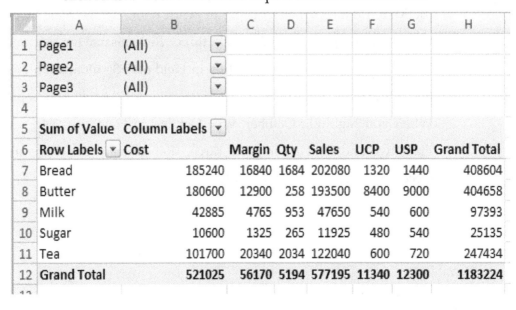

	A	B	C	D	E	F	G	H
1	Page1	(All) ▾						
2	Page2	(All) ▾						
3	Page3	(All) ▾						
4								
5	**Sum of Value**	**Column Labels** ▾						
6	**Row Labels** ▾	Cost	Margin	Qty	Sales	UCP	USP	**Grand Total**
7	Bread	185240	16840	1684	202080	1320	1440	408604
8	Butter	180600	12900	258	193500	8400	9000	404658
9	Milk	42885	4765	953	47650	540	600	97393
10	Sugar	10600	1325	265	11925	480	540	25135
11	Tea	101700	20340	2034	122040	600	720	247434
12	**Grand Total**	**521025**	**56170**	**5194**	**577195**	**11340**	**12300**	**1183224**

Fig 17.28

Under Page1, you can select the month and the output will be adjusted automatically.

Under page2, you can choose which quarter, 1st, 2nd,3rd or 4th and the system will summarize the results of three months representing the quarter you selected. Remember, if you are running the quarterly report, you must select All under Page1

If you like to see the result of 1st or 2nd half of the year, click all under Pages 1 and 2 and select the 1st half to display the total from January to June or 2nd to display the total from July to December.

You may decide to hide USP and UCP.

PIVOTCHART

PivotChart is very similar to PivotTable, I will assume that you have done a comprehensive study of PivotTable above. While PivotTable consolidates or summarizes your data, PivotChart graph the summarized data. As earlier mentioned, they are both similar. PivotChart summarizes the data before drawing the graph. You can have a single range PivotChart or multiple ranges PivotChart like the PivotTable and the modes of accessing the two are similar.

Let's repeat the example we use under Multiple Ranges PivotTable Report we just concluded to prepare a PivotChart by following the steps below:

1. Press Alt + D and touch P to display the PivotTable wizard
2. Select "Multiple Consolidated Ranges" and PivotChart (with PivotTable) and click Next. This will take you to Step 2a
3. Select "I will create the page fields" and click Next to take you to step 2b

4. Click inside "Range" in step 2b and select the range by highlighting cells A2:G7 in the first worksheet

5. Click "Add" and the following appears under All Ranges: 'Sheet1'!$A$2:$G$7

Repeat steps 4 and 5 until you have selected all the ranges in the twelve worksheets.

6. Select 3 under "How many page fields do you want?" and your screen should look like this:

Fig 17.29

7. Highlight the cell that corresponds with your data for January. Type January inside Field one, type 1st Quarter inside Field two and type 1st Half inside field three. Highlight February data and type February in Field one, 1st Quarter in field two and 1st Half in Field three. Repeat same for March data. When you get to April data, change Field two to 2nd Quarter and repeat 1st Half in Field three. Repeat same for May and June. When you highlight July, type July in Field one, 3rd Quarter in Field two and 2nd Half in Field three and repeat same for August and September. When you highlight October, type October in Field one, 3rd

Quarter in Field two and 2nd Half in Field three. Repeat same for November and December and your screen should be similar to this:

Fig 17.30

8.   Click Next to go to Step 3. Select where you like your report to be and click Finish. Your PivotTable Report should look like this:

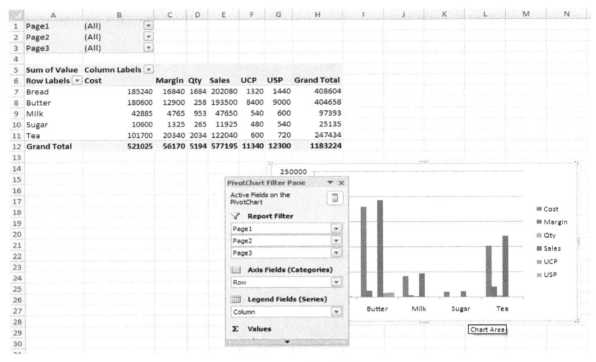

	A	B	C	D	E	F	G	H	I	J	K	L	M	N
1	Page1	(All)												
2	Page2	(All)												
3	Page3	(All)												
4														
5	Sum of Value	Column Labels												
6	Row Labels	Cost		Margin	Qty	Sales	UCP	USP	Grand Total					
7	Bread	185240		16840	1684	202080	1320	1440	408604					
8	Butter	180600		12900	258	193500	8400	9000	404658					
9	Milk	42885		4765	953	47650	540	600	97393					
10	Sugar	10600		1325	265	11925	480	540	25135					
11	Tea	101700		20340	2034	122040	600	720	247434					
12	Grand Total	521025		56170	5194	577195	11340	12300	1183224					

Fig 17.31

Page1 (cell B1) displays All and the 12 months. If you select any month, the PivotTable Report and PivotChart will display that month only.

Page2 (cell B2) displays 1st to 4th quarter but for it to work properly, select all on page1 and pick any quarter on page2 and both your PivotTable Report and the PivotChart Report will automatically reflect the quarter selected.

Once you are on a PivotChart, your menu will reflect 4 additional items vis: Design, Layout, Format and Analysis.

Design: The Design is grouped into:

- **Type** - where you can change the type of chart or save your current chart as a template
- **Data** – which enables you to reselect the data for the chart or switch rows and columns. Note however that under PivotChart, you cannot switch

Row/column. If you click select data, the screen below will appear. If you are using a PivotChart, you may not be able to make any modification here.

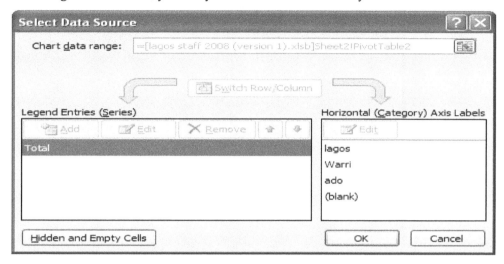

Fig 17.31

- **Chart Layouts** – Under Chart Layouts, you have several layouts to pick to make your chart look attractive. What you pick is what you get.
- **Chart Styles** – Made up of various color combinations and outlooks. You simply click anyone of your choice and your chart reflects your choice.

Layout: The Layout has been grouped into Current Selection, Insert, Labels, Axes, Background, Analysis and Properties.

- **Current Selection** – Once a part of your chart is selected, you can format that part by clicking format selection or reset to match style. For instance, if you click Format Selection, the screen that will be displayed depends on the part of the chart you have selected e.g.

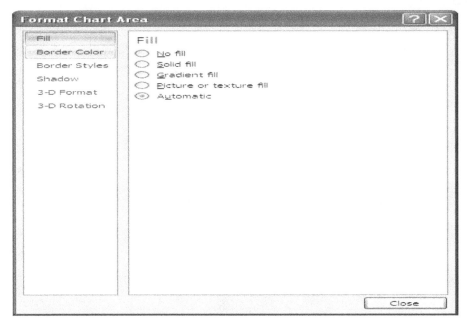

Fig 17.32

You can as well click on "Reset to Match Style" to reset all your format to match the style of chart selected.

- **Insert** – Enables you to insert picture, shapes, text boxes, etc.
- **Labels** – Enable you to enter Chart Titles, Axis Titles, Legend, Data Labels, Data Table, etc
- **Axes** – Take care of Axes and Gridlines
- **Background** – Enables you to set background, change chart wall, apply 3-Dimentional effects or even change the chart floor.
- **Analysis** – Where you can include Trend line, lines, error bars, etc
- **Properties** – Where you can change the chart name

Format: The Format is also grouped into Current Selection, Shape Styles, WordArt Styles, Arrange and Size.

- **Current Selection** – Same under the Layout earlier discussed.

- **Shape Styles** – You have various styles to beautify your chart. Once selected, your chart is automatically formatted to the selected style. Under shape styles, you also have Shape fill that automatically fill the background of your chart with selected color, shape outline that draws an outline using your selected color and shape effects.

- **WordArt Styles** – Give you the opportunities to choose from various WordArt available to beautify you chart. You can also click on Quick Styles and select from the numerous options available. You may decide to fill the character with the color of your choice under the text fill, text effect or text outline

- **Arrange** – You have the selection pane where you can select specific part of your chart and arrange them to your taste

- **Size** – Enables you increase or decrease the size of the chart.

Notes:

18

Using Objects and Graphics

Introduction

There are various objects you can insert in Excel. These include pictures, smart art, clip art, etc. All these items are grouped together under Insert Menu from the main menu.

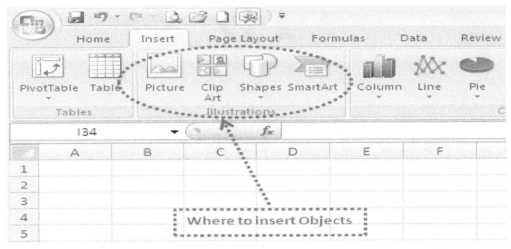

Fig 18.0

Once you click on pictures, a dialogue box will appear displaying all the pictures in the current directory.

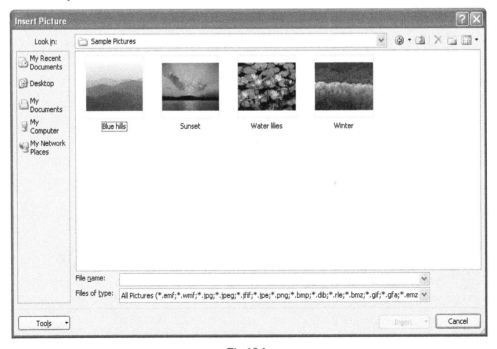

Fig 18.1

Click on your desired picture to insert the picture and a Picture Tool will automatically appear as a new menu that will enable you format your picture.

The Picture tool is organized in four groups:

a) Adjust: Under this option, you can modify your picture by setting the brightness, contrast, recolor, compress, change or reset picture

b) Picture Styles: Under this option, you can select the background, the frame, the shape of the picture, etc.

c) Arrange: You can set other preferences, arrange, align, rotate or decide how the picture flows with the text or cell.

d) Size: You can set the height, the width or even crop the picture to your desired choice.

Insert one of the pictures above and format it to the one below:

Fig 18.2

How do you achieve this? Follow the steps below:

a) Click on **Insert** and select **pictures**

b) Locate where you have sample pictures and select Sunset. The original picture appears like this:

Fig 18.3

I have labeled part of the picture (A), (B), (C) and (D)

A – Enables you to rotate the picture sideways

B – Enables you to resize the picture with exact precision. With this, the picture will not be distorted in terms of height and width

C – You can drag from here to reduce the width of the picture

D – You can drag from here to reduce the height of the picture

c) Highlight the picture and click on "Dark frame black" under picture styles

Fig 18.4

d) Under picture shape, click on hexagon

e) Under picture effects, click on reflection and select Full Reflection, 8pt offset

Clip Art:

Clip Art is a single piece of ready-made art, often appearing as a bitmap or a combination of drawn shapes. In Microsoft Excel, we have collections of clip art and drawings that you can automatically insert in a document to illustrate a specific concept. To insert a Clip Art, click on Clip Art under the Insert menu. A dialogue box will appear as follows:

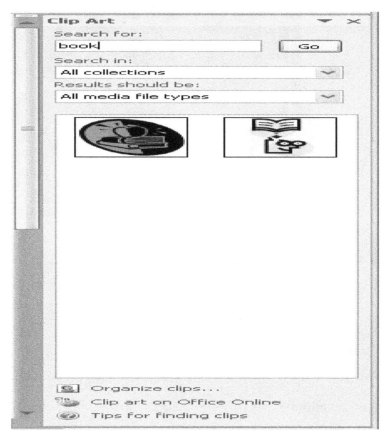

Fig 18.5

You can search for clips by typing common word like book. You can also restrict your search by clicking on the "Search in: " and picking the specific collection and it is also possible to restrict the media file types.

If you click on organize clips, the following will be displayed:

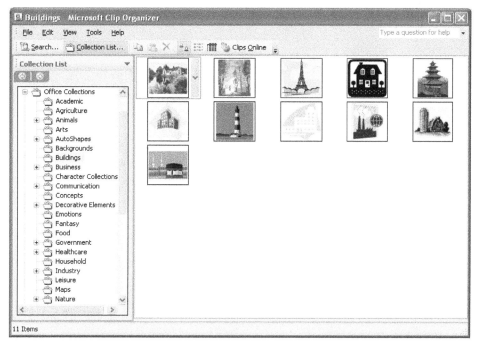

Fig 18.6

With this, you can pick the collection list from the left and the collection will display as shown above.

All other things remain the same as earlier discussed under pictures above.

Shapes:

In Microsoft Excel, there are tons of ready-made shapes such as lines, arrows, callouts, etc that you can automatically insert in a worksheet. This saves you a lot of time to concentrate on more important tasks than drawing your own object. When you click on Shapes under the Insert menu, a screen will be displayed for you to pick your required shapes. The shapes have been grouped into Recently Used Shapes, Lines, Rectangles, Basic Shapes, Block Arrows, Equation Shapes, Flow Charts, Stars and Banners and Callouts.

Once you click on any of the shapes, A + sign appears. At this point, you can hold down the left button of your mouse and drag the shape to your required size. A Drawing Tool main menu appears on the Ribbon with the Format options. The Format is arranged in five groups vis:

a) Insert Shapes: where you can change or insert a new shape

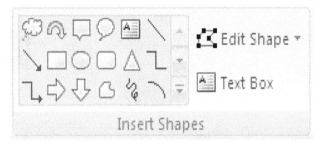

Fig 18.7

b) Shape Styles: where you can select from a ready-made styles and your shape will inherit the format automatically. Such styles include the color, the outline, the shape effect, etc

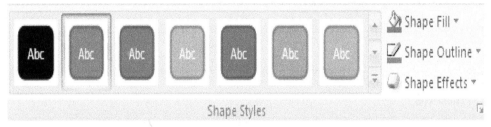

Fig 18.8

c) WordArt Styles: for styles of the associated text. Here you may decide to pick regular text, text with 3-dimensional background, text with outline, etc.

Fig 18.8

d) Arrange: whether you want to bring the shape in front or send it to the back, whether you want to rotate the shape, align it, etc.

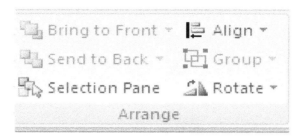

Fig 18.9

Under the selection pane, you can select each shape, rearrange or reorder and even decide the visibility of the shape.

e) Size: for you to increase or reduce the size of the shape

Fig 18.10

SmartArt

SmartArt gives you the opportunity of designing and using more complex graphics in Microsoft Excel. Such graphics include Organization Chart, Venn Diagram, etc.

Once you click on SmartArt, it displays the following:

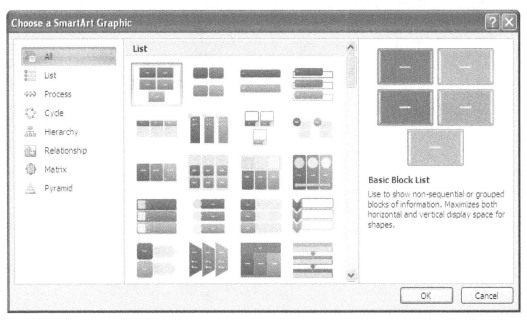

Fig 18.11

On the left hand side, you have the various groups while you have the list of items under each group on the right. Click the group on the left and highlight your selection on the right and click OK.

At this point, the SmartArt will be inserted for you to edit and modify as required. A SmartArt tool will appear with both the Design and Format menu. The Design menu is arranged in four groups:

1) Create Graphics

   You can add additional shape to your SmartArt, move shapes left to right or vice versa, promote or demote, etc.

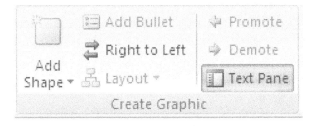

Fig 18.12

2) Layouts

The layouts enable you to choose from a ready-made design. It is similar to the phrase "what you see is what you get" and it is very simple to achieve

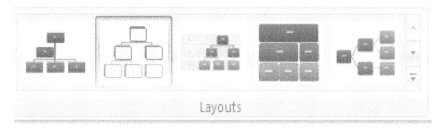

Fig 18.13

Once you click on any of the layouts, your SmartArt inherits the properties of the shape.

3) SmartArt Styles

The SmartArt Styles consist of various styles where you can pick from. You can also change the color of your SmartArt.

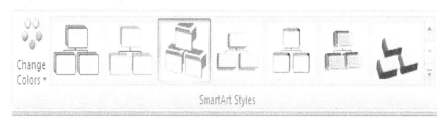

Fig 18.13

4) Reset

Reset will simply return the default setting of your SmartArt.

The Format menu is similar to the one earlier discussed under Pictures.

If you right click on your SmartArt, you can also format, reset and set some of the properties earlier discussed.

Notes:

19

The Lookups

Introduction

The LOOKUP functions can be very useful in extracting information from various worksheets into your current worksheet.

It is another powerful function in Excel that can be used to find information or reduce time spent in entering data. Assuming you have a very large table or arrays of information, finding or locating value can be a very difficult task.

VLOOKUP

A typical scenario where VLOOKUP will be of tremendous assistance is when you are given several pieces of papers containing sales from a retail supermarket that has several stores in many location with identical products, unit price and other information to form a workbook. In that situation, you could spend several hours, days, weeks or months to achieve this but with VLOOKUP function, you will spend less. To achieve the goal, you could:

1. Set up the first sheet that will contain unique identification number or code for each of the products, description, unit of measure, unit selling price, etc.

2. Set up another sheet that will contain the information about each store with unique code

3. Start creating your data. With VLOOKUP, you will no longer need to type a long product code, warehouse, etc. All you simply need to do is to type the code of the product and the product description or any other information required comes up automatically.

Syntax: VLOOKUP(value to lookup, range name or array, column to pick, false)

Let's use the following data to practice this function.

Somolu

Product	UOM	Unit Price	Quantity Sold	Value
Sugar	Pkt	250.00	60.00	15,000.00

Product	UOM	Unit Price	Quantity Sold	Value
Salt	50kg	1,500.00	40.00	60,000.00
Milk	Each	20.00	4,500.00	90,000.00
Flour	50kg	6,000.00	15.00	90,000.00
Rice	50kg	6,000.00	450.00	2,700,000.00
Rice	25kg	3,000.00	500.00	1,500,000.00
Rice	10kg	600.00	1,300.00	780,000.00
Yeast	5kg	350.00	1,000.00	350,000.00
				5,585,000.00

Lagos Island

Product	UOM	Unit Price	Quantity Sold	Value
Salt	25kg	750.00	250.00	187,500.00
Milk	Each	20.00	600.00	12,000.00
Sugar	Pkt	250.00	700.00	175,000.00
Flour	50kg	6,000.00	500.00	3,000,000.00
Rice	50kg	6,000.00	45.00	270,000.00
Rice	25kg	3,000.00	750.00	2,250,000.00
Rice	10kg	600.00	650.00	390,000.00
Yeast	5kg	350.00	2,000.00	700,000.00
				6,984,500.00

Table 19.0

Let's assume the above information is on pieces of papers from the two locations and you could have several of such to input into Excel. If you have to enter the product, unit of measure, the unit selling price every time a product is sold, it will take quite a number of hours to get the job done. With VLOOKUP, you can achieve this with ease.

From the information given, we can create a template worksheet that will contain product code, description, unit of measure and unit selling price while other sheets will contain the information with a VLOOKUP to pick the correct product once a code is entered. Let's create a master worksheet with the following information:

	A	B	C	D	E
1	Product Code	Product	Unit of Measure	Unit Price	
2	KAR001	Sugar	Pkt	250.00	
3	KAR005	Salt	50kg	1,500.00	
4	KAR006	Milk	Each	20.00	
5	KAR007	Flour	50kg	6,000.00	
6	KAR010	Rice	50kg	6,000.00	
7	KAR011	Rice	25kg	3,000.00	
8	KAR012	Rice	10kg	600.00	
9	KAR020	Yeast	5kg	350.00	
10	KAR005	Salt	25KG	750.00	
11					

Fig 19.0

From the above, we have created the master sheet with unique code for each product. Let us create a range name for the master sheet and we will call it "MASTER" (see Creating Range Name and The Importance) for information on how to create range name.

We can now enter Somolu information with ease. Insert a new worksheet and call it Somolu. Enter the headings, copy cells A2 to A10 from master and paste it to somolu (A3)

	A	B	C	D	E	F
1			Somolu			
2	Product Code	Product	Unit of Measure	Unit Price	Quantity Sold	Value
3	KAR001					-
4	KAR005					-
5	KAR006					-
6	KAR007					-
7	KAR010					-
8	KAR011					-
9	KAR012					-
10	KAR020					-
11	KAR005					-
12						

Fig 19.1

Enter the following in the cells listed below

B3   =VLOOKUP(A3,MASTER,2,FALSE)

You are actually searching for the value in Cell A3 which is currently blank

MASTER: The range name we just created

2: we are picking information from the second column of MASTER

False: Look for the exact information, do not use similar value. This is very important where a range is not arranged in alphabetical order.

C3   VLOOKUP(A3,MASTER,3,FALSE)

C4   VLOOKUP(A3,MASTER,4,FALSE)

Highlight cells B3, C3 and D3; press Ctrl+C to copy. Highlight cells B4 to B11 and press Ctrl+V to paste. The product name, unit of measure and unit price will automatically appear. The only information you need to enter will be the quantity sold.

 Repeat the above for Lagos Island and you will be amazed at the time spent to complete the exercise.

As earlier mentioned, VLOOKUP is a powerful tool. It is therefore advisable to practice with several tables to grasp the function. You can combine the function with other function to build powerful queries and conditional statements.

The HLOOKUP

This is similar to VLOOKUP. The major difference is that while VLOOKUP checks columns, the HLOOKUP checks rows i.e. horizontally. Syntax and all other things are similar. The" V" in VLOOKUP stands for vertical while the "H" in HLOOKUP stands for horizontal.

The LOOKUP

This is ordinary LOOKUP without the V or the H. We will not lay emphasis on this because of the limitations but for the purpose of learning, the syntax is:

=LOOKUP(Value, vector to search, result vector)

Value = the value you are searching for

Vector to search = the range you are searching

Result vector = the range containing the result you are looking for

Assuming you have 1 to 20 in column A and you have names of individuals in column B, you may want to know the name of an individual corresponding to 15. The lookup formula will look like this:

=LOOKUP(15,A1:A20,B1:B20)

Excel will look for 15 in column A and return the value corresponding to it in column B. It is however important to note that you data must be sorted in ascending order for lookup to be accurate.

The MATCH FUNCTION

This function simply returns the value corresponding to the position of the item you are looking up. The syntax is:

=MATCH(value to find, range to search, type)

Value to find = the value you are looking for

Range to search = the range where the value can be found

Type: This is optional and can either be -1, 0 or 1

> -1: Match looks for the smallest value that is greater than or equal to the "value to find". If the range is not in descending order, you are likely going to get an error.

> 0: The exact value. Range to search can be in any order.

> 1: Finds the largest value that is less than or equal to. If the range is not in ascending order, you are likely going to get an error.

Match Function will be more useful when you are looking for the position of a value in array rather than the value itself.

20

Macros &
Automation

Introduction

One of the best ways of achieving high level of efficiency is by automating tasks that are repetitive in nature. With automation, such tasks can be performed faster and are more reliable than performing the task manually. Many thought that only programmers can automate task and have not actually made any attempt to learn the process of automation. This chapter will discuss how automation can be done in Excel without going too deep into programming.

Think about those repetitive tasks that take time to accomplish and analyze the tasks step by step. Let's analyze one of the functions of a Treasury Officer who pays suppliers daily in an environment where automation is not in place. He is expected to do the following:

- Extracts the invoices due for payment from the ledger into Excel
- Sorts the invoices by Vendor
- Calculates the total by vendor
- Issues cheque and pays the invoices
- Summarizes all the cheque issued to generate his Cash Register
- Etc.

The above functions can be regarded as routine functions as he goes through the same process the next day. To reduce the time spent in performing this type of tasks, one can automate the processes in Microsoft Excel by recording the processes using macro. The set up procedure may take more time for the first time but subsequent processing will be a matter of pressing a button to perform the tasks. The act of automation involves recording, editing and running a Macro. A Macro can be described as recorded steps that assist you in performing some specific tasks with little or no user intervention. Following are the steps required in automation:

- Record Macro
- Edit Macro

- Create Shortcut or Button for your macro
- Save your File

Recording Macro

Macro icon can be located under View from the standard menu. Once you click on Macros, you are presented with three options: View Macros, Record macros, Use Relative References.

Fig 20.0

Click Record Macro and the following dialog box will appear:

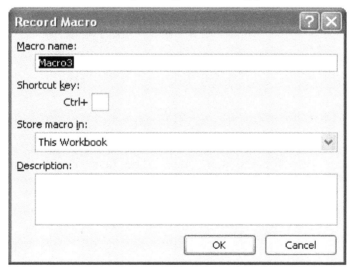

Fig 20.1

- **Macro name:** The name you intend to assign to the Macro

- **Shortcut Key:** Assign any small or cap letter to the macro. Note that this will override the key combination earlier discussed in Chapter 3

- **Store Macro in :** You can store your macro in Personal Macro workbook, the current workbook or in a new workbook

- **Description:** Full description of what the macro does. This can be useful where you have so many macros in a worksheet or workbook

Once you have finished entering that information, click Ok to proceed or Cancel to disregard your entries.

If you click Ok, your keystrokes will be recorded by Microsoft Excel until you click Stop Recoding.

To stop recording, click Macro again and click Stop Recording. Your Macro is saved either for modification or use.

Let us assume that we have a worksheet with the following data:

	A	B	C	D	E
1					
2			XYZ LIMITED		
3					
4			STAFF INFORMATION		
5	Code	Name	Date of Birth	Sex	Home Address
6	XYZ001	Jack James	1-Jan-1990	Male	13 Jeunjeje Street, Agbara, Lagos, Nigeria
7	XYZ002	Jack Julie	12-May-2000	Female	1a Ilasa Road, Ikogosi, Ekiti, Nigeria
8	XYZ003	John Bull	6-Feb-1998	Male	12 Ilabere Layout, Otta, Ogun, Nigeria
9	XYZ004	Black Horse	5-Apr-1967	Male	5 Soyombo Road, Ibadan, Oyo, Nigeria
10	XYZ005	Dale Brown	9-Sep-2005	Female	8 Diobu Lane, Port Harcourt, Rivers, Nigeria
11					

Fig 20.2

Remember that the data could run into columns and thousands of rows. We are going to create separate copies for the staff files. The task means that we are printing thousands of copies depending on the number of employees we have (in this case just 5). Below is the sample of the final output for each employee:

XYZ LIMITED

STAFF INFORMATION

Staff Code	**XYZ003**
Name:	JOHN BULL
Date of Birth	6-Feb-1998
Sex	Male
Home Address:	12 Ilabere Layout, Otta, Ogun, Nigeria

Fig 20.3

How best can we accomplish this if we have up to 3000 employees with more information than we presently have on the above worksheet? Let's ignore all other options and concentrate on using Macro to perform the task. The following are the steps required:

a) Let's name the entire information "data" (see range name if you don't know how to do this).

b) Create another worksheet that looks exactly like your output above (i.e. the second picture). The second sheet should look like this:

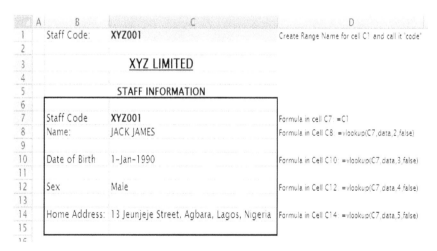

Fig 20.4

You will be using cell C1 for your input and once you enter the staff code on cell C1, cell C7 picks the information and the vlookup formulas in cells C8, C10, C12 and C14 pick up the values from the data table

c)   Set your Print Area to cover B6:B15 and your Print Titles to cover Rows 3:5

d)   Click on Macros and select Record Macro. Complete the dialog box as follows:

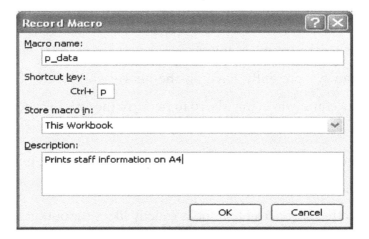

Fig 20.4

e)   Click OK to start recording

f)   Type XYZ001 in cell C1 and Excel completes the other cells automatically

g)   Click Print from the Customized Quick Access Toolbar to print the information for staff XYZ001

h)   Click stop recording. At this point, your macro has been saved and we need to make little modifications to the macro.

Modifying Macro Codes

Click on Macros again and select View Macros.

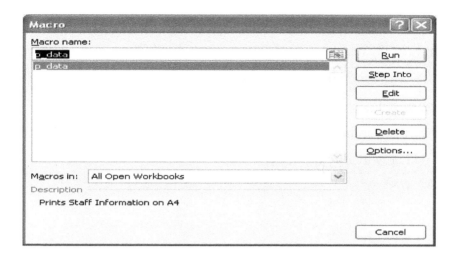

Fig 20.5

Highlight p_data, click Edit and the following screen appears

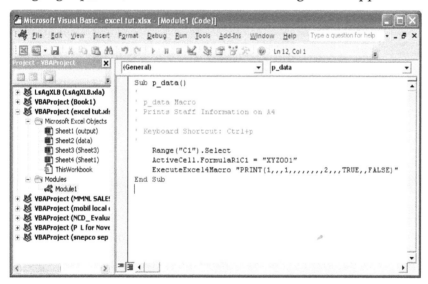

Fig 20.6

On the left hand side are the projects or files opened and on the right are the codes you want to modify.

The Sub marks the beginning of your code and the End Sub marks the end.

Range ("C1").Select means that you selected cell C1

ActiveCell.FormulaR1C1 = "XYZ001" means that you type XYZ001 in the selected range or cell

The next line indicate that you selected Print

We will now modify the above to read

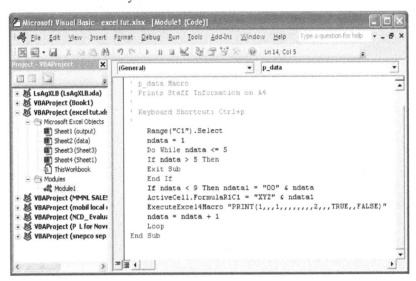

Fig 20.7

I have created two variables called ndata and ndata1. I have also assigned 1 to ndata and used if command to assign value to ndata1

The "if" formula is necessary because I want the system to automatically assign the staff code. Since the pattern is XYZ001, it means if the number is greater than 9, the system should remove 0 and change the code to XYZ010, etc.

Do while ndata<=5 instructs the system to carry out all instructions between the "Do While" and Loop until the value of ndata is greater than 5

Exit Sub means get out of the sub routine once ndata is greater than 5

Loop terminates the Do While instructions

....

...

Loop

You have successfully recorded your Macro for the above project. Let's take it a little bit further by creating a button for it. Follow the steps below:

Creating Control Button

a) Click Controls on the Customized Quick Access Toolbar, then click Insert and the screen below will appear:

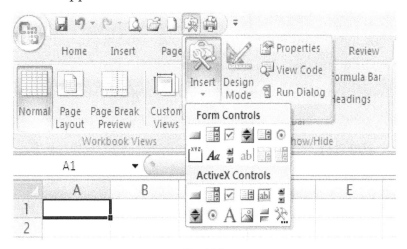

Fig 20.8

b) Click on Button (Form Control)

c) Move your cursor to where you want the Button to be, hold down the left button of your mouse and drag it until you are happy with the size of the Button

d) As soon as you release the mouse, a dialog box appear

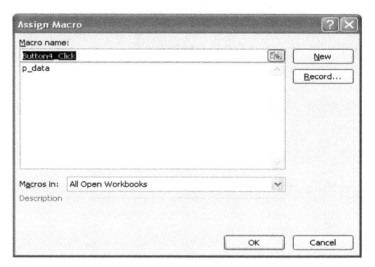

Fig 20.9

This will assist you in assigning your Macro to the Button

e) Highlight the p_data and click OK. At this point, the system has attached your Macro to the Button.

f) Change the default text of the Button by clicking the right button of your mouse on the Button. Click Edit Text and change the text to My Macro.

g) You can also format your control by selecting Format Control instead of Edit Text.

Any time you click the Button, all the employees will be printed.

21

Printing Your Job

You will cover:

- *Introduction*
- *Setting Print Area and Print Titles*
- *Modifying the Print Margins*
- *Inserting the Header and Footer*
- *Changing the Properties of your Printer*
- *Sending your Job to the Printer*

Introduction

Printing your job is a very simple process in Microsoft Excel. It is important to arrange your job properly to reduce wastage such as papers, print inks or tonners, etc.

Following are some of the preliminary steps before printing:

1) Set up Print Area and Print Titles
2) Modify the properties of your printer if required
3) Preview your job
4) Print the file

All this options can be accessed under the Page Layout discussed below. The Page Layout is one of the Main Menu in Microsoft Excel:

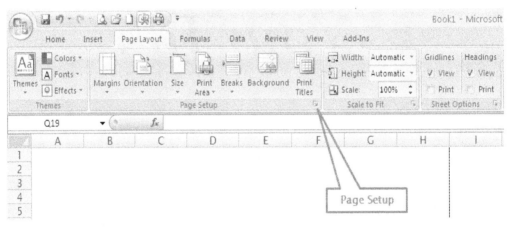

Fig 21.0

Under the Page Layout, we have Themes, Page Setup, Scale to Fit and Sheet Options

Themes:

These are combination of colors, fonts and effects. Whenever you make a change, it affects the entire workbook.

Page Setup:

This enables you to adjust or set the following parameters:

- **Margin:** Under the margin, you have preset margins like the normal, the wide, the narrow or even custom. The custom margin enables you to decide your top, bottom, left and right margins.

- **Orientation:** Here, you will be able to decide whether your print job is going to be in landscape or portrait format.

- **Size:** This comes up with various paper sizes where you can make your selection. In addition, you can decide and customize your desired paper size.

- **Print Area:** To set or clear print area.

- **Breaks:** You can insert a page break or clear page break under Breaks

- **Background:** This enables you to use your desired picture or image as the background of your job.

- **Print Titles:** At times, your print job could span to several pages made up of tables with several columns. If you print such jobs without Print Titles, reading becomes difficult since you may not remember which column holds what. Setting Print Titles will assist you in getting over this. It enables you to specify which rows you intend to print on top of all the pages or the columns you intend to print on the left hand side of all the pages or both rows and columns.

  Print Titles are very important when you are printing multiple pages.

All the options discussed can be accessed by clicking on the arrow marked Page Setup on the diagram above.

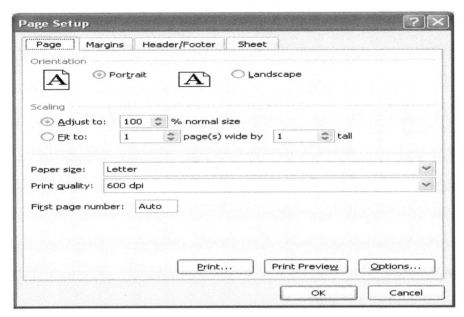

Fig 21.1

There are four tabs under Page Setup.

1) Page:

   Made up of Orientation earlier discussed, Scaling where you can adjust your print job to your desired number of pages; you can select paper size by clicking on the drop down combo; print quality and whether you want the first page to be automatically numbered.

2) Margins: You can set the margins earlier discussed

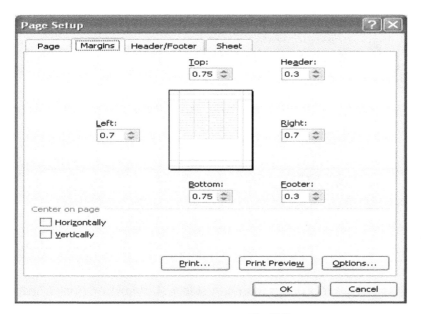

Fig 21.2

In addition to the margins earlier discussed, we have two other options under Center on Page.

- Horizontally: This will ensure that your output is at the center of the page horizontally i.e. left to right.
- Vertically: Your output will be centralized vertically i.e. top to bottom.

3) Header/Footer: This is where you determine what you want on top or bottom of each page apart from the headings. Example of this can be page number, cell reference, name of file, etc.

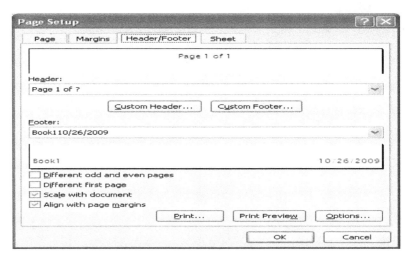

Fig 21.3

- Standard Header/Footer: You can select standard or preset headers and footers from the drop down combo.

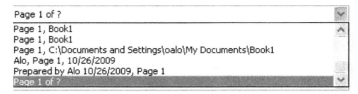

Fig 21.4

You can also use a Custom Header or Footer.

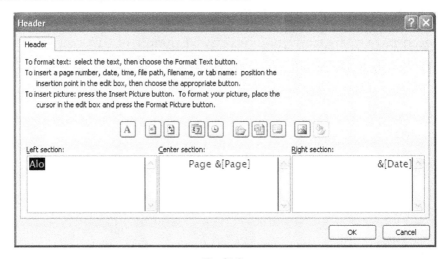

Fig 21.5

You may decide to have your Header or Footer on the left, at the center, on the right or you may even decide to have three different Header or Footer at the same time. If you place your cursor on Icons, you will have an idea of what you can insert.

4) Sheet

Under the Sheet, we have the Print Area earlier discussed, the Print Titles, and some other options:

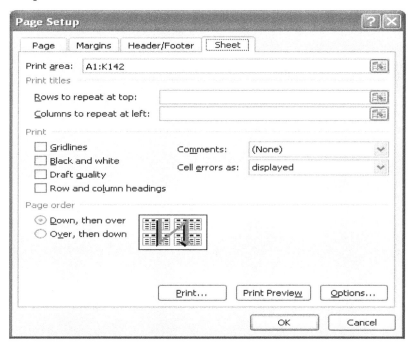

Fig 21.6

You may decide to include the Grid lines, Comments, Cell errors, Row and Column Headings and you can even decide to change your colored worksheet to black and white.

The Page order determines how your job is printed if you have multiple pages.

There are three other buttons under Page Setup:

1) Print: Sends your job to the printer

2) Print Preview: Previews your job so that you can see how it appears before printing

3) Options: enables you to change the properties of your printer before printing your job. The properties include: Draft or quality copy, color management, advanced options, etc.

It is important to know that the options you have will depend on the printer installed and your administrative privileges. If you are restricted, you may not be able to make changes to the Printer options.

It is also important to note that you can access the print options under the Customized Quick Access Toolbar. There you have icons such as Quick Print and Print Preview. Quick Print sends your job to the printer while the preview enables you to view your job before sending it to the printer.

www.ingramcontent.com/pod-product-compliance
Lightning Source LLC
Chambersburg PA
CBHW080400060326
40689CB00019B/4083